ON ASSIGNMENT

SUPPORTING LOVED ONES
THROUGH ADDICTION AND RECOVERY

VIV MARTIN

ISBN: 978-1-962402-04-0

Published by
Lady VLTM Productions, LLC
LadyVLTMProductions@gmail.com

This book is a memoir. It reflects the author's personal experiences to the best of her recollection. Others may remember events differently. Certain names and identifying details have been changed to protect the privacy of individuals. Some conversations or moments have been condensed or reconstructed for clarity and narrative flow, but the essence of the memories and sentiments remains true to the author's journey.

DEDICATION

This book is dedicated to my mentor, Stacey Cooper, for her support, sacred wisdom, and friendship from the day that we met until her passing. May she rest in peace.

ACKNOWLEDGMENTS

First and foremost, I thank God for giving me my story, the courage, the strength, the driving force to tell it, and His unshakable love and leadership. To my parents, Wilton and Geraldine Thomas, thank you for giving me a grounded upbringing filled with love, education, and spirituality. A special thank you to my husband for his influence, his unwavering trust in me and my vision, and for pushing me to strive for excellence.

Thank you to my sisters: Deanne Renard, who assisted me with my first attempt at editing this book and who offered her input on articulating my story to my audience; Shauna Ewens, who listened to my relentless raving about my dream of writing and publishing my book and for her upliftment and reassurance in pursuing my dream; and Dr. Monya Criddle, my youngest sister, who motivated and energized me to keep moving and never give up.

To my children and grandchildren, thank you for granting me the time and space for creativity to flourish. To my many friends and relatives who rallied along the way for me: Juanita Catalon, Elaine Davidson, William Shaw, Maryanne Bertuglia, Carolyn Morris, Salinda Thurman, Dietrich Thomas, Bessie Paris, Betty Roberson, Tony Maldonado, Ruben Townsend, and Kenita (Kay) Townsend, thank you for cheering me on.

And last, but not least, to my editor, Paulette K. Kinnes, and my publisher, Robin Surface, thank you for your assistance in making this book a reality.

CONTENTS

INTRODUCTION

I must have thought to myself a million times that this could not be the husband God chose for me. His loyalty and devotion resembled that of a person incapable of love, faithfulness, and fulfilling sacred vows made before God.

The thought of forsaking all others vanished in a darkened room where I lay on many nights wondering whether my husband had a mistress or some secret life. Twenty years after meeting my husband, Terry Martin, on November 18, 1996, I was certain of the infidelity in our marriage. The culprit behind my wonderment was drugs. And her name? Crack cocaine. Below is an excerpt from the Bible of God's conversation with Hosea concerning his wife Gomer and her infidelity, which aligned with the feelings that cut through my heart on those lonely nights:

> The beginning of the word of the Lord by Hosea. And the Lord said to Hosea, "Go, take unto thee a wife of whoredoms and children of whoredoms... for the land hath committed great whoredom, departing from the Lord. So, he went and took Gomer the daughter of Diblaim; which conceived and bore him a son."
>
> Hosea 1:2-3 (KJV)

> Then the Lord said to me, "Go, again, love a woman who is loved by a lover and is committing adultery, just like the love of the LORD for the children of Israel, who look to other gods and love the raisin cakes of the pagans." So, I brought her for myself for fifteen shekels of silver, and one and one-half homers of barley. And I said to her, "You shall stay with me many days; you shall not play the harlot, nor shall you have a man — so, too, will I be toward you."
>
> Hosea 3:1-3 (NKJV)

After reading the entire book of Hosea in the Bible, these excerpts jumped off the pages as living words and enabled me to see a connection between my husband's drug addiction and Hosea's relationship with his wife. Hosea's love for his wife, Gomer, symbolized God's love for Israel, and Gomer's response to Hosea's love symbolized Israel's response to God. In Hosea 3:1-3 (NKJV), Gomer was a woman who was committing adultery and was referred to, by God, as an adulteress. This symbolization made me wonder how was it possible for Israel to commit adultery against God?

My conclusion was that Israel could not, and that the common interpretation of adultery could not have been applied in the above scriptures. However, what is being implied and what is required is a deeper reflection of the meaning of adultery. The Oxford English Dictionary and Merriam-Webster define adultery as *voluntary sexual intercourse between a married person and a person who is not his or her spouse.* This definition ties adultery to sex and only sex outside of the marriage union.

In considering the symbolizations between God and Israel, I am suggesting that adultery goes beyond sexual intercourse and reveals a greater violation, a violation of one's legal vows and commitment to another person. With this expansion of the definition, adultery becomes all inclusive. It includes all vows/covenant violations, sexual intercourse outside of the marriage, and even embodies the possibility of a person committing adultery against God. This enlarged meaning ties adultery to the marriage commitment and not to sexual intercourse outside of the marriage union alone.

With the new definition of adultery being more inclusive, sexual intercourse outside of a person's marriage becomes one of several means by which adultery may be executed. Vows/covenant violations are massive because the promises made within the union are involved. When these pledges are violated, loyalty, faithfulness, and trust are jeopardized such that they may have a similar impact on the marriage as one person having sexual intercourse outside the marriage.

Whether I am cheated on verbally or mentally or physically abused or forsaken/abandoned because someone or something was placed before me, the feelings generated by such treatment may now be contemplated under the expanded definition of adultery. This broadens the scope and creates other forms of adultery to include the symbolization of God referring to Gomer as an adulteress and Israel committing adultery against God.

God requires that we be devoted, constant, and dedicated, forsaking all others for Him. That same requirement is the epitome of God's strategy incorporated into the foundation of the institution of marriage. God instructed man to leave his father's house and to cleave unto his wife. The apostle Paul, in the book of 1 Corinthians, imparts wisdom and knowledge concerning the married and the unmarried.

> *But I want you to be without care. He who is unmarried cares for the things of the Lord — how he may please the Lord. But he who is married cares about the things of the world — how he may please his wife. There is a difference also between a wife and a virgin. The unmarried woman cares about the things of the Lord, that she may be holy both in body and in spirit. But she who is married cares about the things of the world — how she may please her husband.*
> 1 Corinthians 7:32-35 (NKJV)

This scripture illustrates how God has approved for husband and wife to focus more on one another, even above how they may please Him. This doesn't mean that husband and wife should not please the Lord. It emphasizes the level of importance that God has placed on the most critical elements in a marriage.

It is ironic that, in general, I am loyal by nature. I am 62 years old, and I have had two professional jobs in my entire adult life. I stayed at my first job for eight years before the company laid me off. I was at my last job for twenty-six and a half years before retiring on May 31, 2022, with a full pension.

I have had four or five real boyfriends, all of whom either left me, or God removed them from my life. I have had one husband, whom I dated for six years and to whom I have been married for more than twenty-two years.

I've had my closest friends for more than twenty-five years, except for God. He has been my friend since I turned 14 years old, though I have been His friend for all my life.

So, where did I go wrong? How did I end up with a husband who didn't appear capable of loving me in the same manner in which he received love from me? Thoughts like *Why is my husband a drug addict? Why is my husband not a doctor, a lawyer, an Indian Chief, or an effective demonstrator of his feelings?* cartwheeled through my mind every single day.

I was sure that I was not alone in this predicament, and I knew that these could not be desolate questions rolling around in my head waiting for answers from God and within. It has taken twenty years, but God has answered my prayers and has revealed to me in bite-sized pieces the purpose behind my life's voyage, the paths that I have taken over my lifetime. The obstacles, the adversities and hurdles, and the lessons that I have learned permit me now to teach and extend encouragement to others. This is the course and the purpose that I now call *My Journey*.

I am convinced that God's perspective is that drug addiction has paralyzed many of His people. Those who support addicts, which include spouses, children, parents, relatives, and friends are all afflicted and affected by their loved ones' addiction. It is the crying out of these people that God hears, as well as the voice of the addict himself.

This book is intended to invigorate, galvanize, reassure, engage, and bring comfort to those who feel like they are alone. God promises never to leave us. And, though I may not know all readers on a personal level, I do know the pain of drug addiction, which is why my heart goes out to drug addicts and even more so to those who support them.

CHAPTER ONE

DOWN MEMORY LANE

I can't count the number of times that I've questioned God about His reasons for bestowing upon me a husband with drug issues and the other circumstances that I have faced, only to hear and feel stillness as a response. Could this be a sign of God not listening, ignoring me, or preoccupation with grander divine matters? I simply couldn't figure it out.

So, I asked myself and my closest friend and spiritual advisor, Stacey, why me and she answered, "Well, if not you, then who?"

Could this have been God's resolve and the motive behind the mute response? Perhaps His quiet response spoke volumes in conveying disappointment in my lack of trust, thus refusing to dignify the question with an answer.

My next prayer focused primarily on His forgiveness for not trusting Him. During that quiet time, God's omnipresence and sovereign grace drizzled through me like a refreshing rain on a hot summer day as He took me down memory lane to my childhood, my adolescent years, and my earlier young adult experiences.

I am a native of New Orleans, Louisiana, I was raised by wonderful parents. My God-fearing mother taught my three sisters and me to treat others the way that we would like to be treated and never to minimize the plight of the poor and underprivileged because it was only by the grace of God that we were not in a similar situation.

She raised us in church and ensured that my older sister and I participated in whatever activity in which the teachers at the church needed children to participate. If a donkey for the Christmas play was needed, my mother had two, my sister and me.

Volunteering had a different meaning in our house, and useless moaning only led to us being voluntold to do whatever was on the roster for that day. By the time that my two younger sisters reached an age where they were voluntold for church activities, we had moved to the suburbs, New Orleans East, and the distance from church made it inconvenient for my mother to haul us to every church event or activity.

I am thankful that my mother introduced us to God by raising my sisters and me according to God's principles. Doing so gave us the best gift that a mother could give to her children, a solid foundation.

Even with that solid foundation, I sowed my appreciable wild oats. While in junior high school, friends introduced me to smoking cigarettes and marijuana. We hid in the bathroom, passed cigarettes between us, all while thinking how cool we were. Many of the other kids smoked, and, at that age, the need to fit in and earn approval from others seemed important.

If only I had known, then, what I know now! The decision to smoke while in junior high presented the entry point to a life of addiction for me in the form of smoking cigarettes. But God uses both pleasurable and horrific experiences, as well as successes and failures, in life to execute His purpose. Having an addiction of my own has played a critical role in my comprehension of and my perspective on addiction.

High school bought with it more trials, tests, and struggles. I needed to be accepted, while at the same time I needed to be my own person. Most of the neighborhood teenagers who impressed me smoked marijuana and cigarettes and drank beer and wine. As it turned out, the perceived differences between us didn't exist because our search for receptiveness landed us on common ground, and the best ways to illustrate that embrace involved smoking and drinking.

When I was 18, my boyfriend, Eric Ratleff, whom I met on a blind date and ended up dating for a couple of years, and I welcomed the biggest blessing from God, a baby girl. Born on December 14, 1981, I named her Erika Monique Thomas. Though my romantic relationship with Eric ended, we maintained contact and an intermittent friendship due to Eric's own battles and difficulties with addiction. In 2008, Eric finally overcame his addiction. Our friendship developed into a closer bond as he, Erika, and Erika's two children worked on advancing their own personal relationships. Sometime in the summer of 2022 Eric's health deteriorated, and he died on October 27, 2023, from liver complications.

With my pregnancy, God had found a way to slow me down because had it not been for my pregnancy, I would have gone to California to attend college at the University of California, Los Angeles (UCLA). I had always dreamed of moving to California, so going to school in California would have been the best avenue to achieve this goal.

After finding out that I was pregnant, those plans came to a sudden and immediate halt. Instead, I attended night classes at the local community college, Delgado Community College, in New Orleans. I can only imagine what I would have been like in California, foot loose and fancy free, willing to experiment with any drug that did not involve needles to stay connected to the social scene.

Between the time that I graduated from high school in May of 1981 and the time that I graduated from Delgado in the spring of 1985, I experimented with a number of drugs. I snorted cocaine, laced cocaine in cigarettes and weed, popped black mollies, snorted PCP powder, and smoked angel dust.

I smoked the angel dust by mistake not by choice, not that that mattered much. I thought that the canister out of which I snuck the joint only had weed in it. Years later, when talking to my uncle, he told me what I had actually smoked was a joint laced with a drug called angel dust, a powerful hallucinogenic drug, developed as an anesthetic in the 1950s but discontinued for human medical use due to severe side effects in 1965. He told me he had always wondered what had happened to that joint. He thought that one of his sons had stolen it. We laughed for hours and hours about that one!

The effects from smoking that joint stopped me from sneaking another rolled joint out of my uncle's canister without talking to him first. I will never forget that night. After taking a pull off the joint a couple of times, I saw one roach and thought that I had roaches slithering all over me. I ran around the corner to Eric's house screaming that millions of roaches were crawling on me.

He exclaimed, "Girl, you be trippin'! Ain't no damn roaches on you! What the hell you been smoking?"

I also smoked crack for the first time involuntarily. Bill Jenkins, a friend about whom I will go into greater detail in the next chapter, as a joke, placed some crack in a crack pipe, and when I inquired about this, he indicated that it was weed mixed with powdered cocaine, which he called lacing, in the pipe. Before this experience, I had heard of crack, but I had never seen it, so I did not question his explanation.

After two or three hits, I passed the pipe and pretended like I had acquired a level of high that I had not. The next time that I smoked it, I figured that since the first time was such a non-event and that perhaps I had done it wrong, I should give it a second try.

For some reason, once again, no buzz. Bill appeared to have been feeling the effects of the drug, but no matter how many times I hit it, I didn't feel any different. I couldn't figure out why it had no effect on me.

Those two experiences left me not liking crack cocaine. My drug of choice became weed, because at least with weed, I did feel the effects.

I continued down this path of self-destruction for five or six years without any thought as to how it could affect my future. It wasn't until after I graduated from Delgado Community College and moved to San Jose, California, on January 15, 1988, that I stopped experimenting with different drugs.

I decided to move to San Jose after my high school friend, Cassanova, moved there. Over the course of Cassanova living there for a few years, he called me periodically to check on me and encouraged me to visit him in San Jose. I always told him that one day I would come.

I wanted to move to California, not necessarily San Jose, but somewhere in California because at the age of 10, my aunt Bobbie took my sister, Deanne, two of my cousins, and me, to Los Angeles to visit her friend, Ms. McFerguson. I loved the atmosphere and the beautiful weather, so after that visit, I dreamed of moving to California one day. It wasn't until Cassanova moved to San Jose that the opportunity presented itself, again, after my plans to go to UCLA fell apart.

I needed money to move to San Jose. I wasn't working at the time, so after discussing my predicament with my uncle, he suggested that I could work at his mechanic's shop for a few weeks, which included duties such as answering the phone, picking up lunch and auto parts, and going to the racetrack to bet on a horse or two for him. In less than a month I had earned enough to buy a one-way ticket to San Jose and to have a few dollars of spending money. However, once I got there, I would need a job.

At 24 years of age, I realized that God had given me a major responsibility, Erika, to move me forward with the plans that He knew would develop, teach, and prosper in me as my faith and trust in Him grew. So, on January 15, 1988, I moved to San Jose. After staying with Cassanova for three months, I moved into my own two-bedroom, one-bath apartment in the same apartment complex in which I had lived with Cassanova.

While in San Jose, I worked for National Semiconductor, and I completed my education by attending the University of San Francisco, where I obtained a bachelor's degree in organizational behavior. Even with this accomplishment, I continued to smoke weed. I didn't consider myself addicted to weed or anything of the sort. I just liked the energy that smoking gave me. After smoking a joint, I could clean the house to spotlessness and then relax as I watched a movie on TV.

While in San Jose, I kept in contact with three of my closest friends from New Orleans, Bill Jenkins, Ricky Flores, and Lylah Bastion. What they had in common, other than being my friends with whom I engaged in doing drugs, their drug usage escalated, and all three of them became addicted to crack cocaine.

My closest and most loyal friend, my funniest friend, and my coolest friend, all addicted to crack cocaine, but not me. Why? Was it luck, or had God spared me? And if He had spared me, for what purpose?

More than twenty years later God opened my eyes as to why I didn't feel the effects of crack cocaine and why He chose to spare me from such an addiction. He unveiled to me that an addiction to crack cocaine was not meant to be a part of my voyage. Instead, my involvement suited me best as a part of the support system for those who became addicted to crack cocaine. And for me to be effective, I needed to be subjected to it, yet protected from it, to avoid being judgmental and critical of those who became addicted.

My experience with crack cocaine enabled me to know that being spared from drug addiction wasn't a result of me being smarter or stronger than anyone else because, after all, I too had tried using it a couple of times. God's power, His plans, and His purpose for my life placed me as a member of the support system for drug addicts. As a source of strength, my role included offering spiritual support, guidance, and the use of spiritual warfare, a subject I will dive deeper into in later chapters. Through this role, glory and honor would be brought to God.

In retrospect, I can see that God used my three friends to lay the foundation and set the stage for my ability to be open about drug addiction. I did not realize it at the time, but with each of my friends, he used their personalities and lives to teach me not to be judgmental and to learn that drug addiction is not about the person. It runs deeper than that because addiction does not care who it impacts.

I loved my friends. Their lives and my life intertwined with more similarities than differences. The most profound lesson that I learned from my friends is how addiction changes personalities, characters, and normalcies in what seems like the blink of an eye, though in most cases, it happens over the course of years of drug use.

In the next three chapters I impart insights from the lives of my three friends so that readers may see their true personalities, characters, and hearts and the impact that their addictions had on them.

I am confident that reading these stories will help readers to grasp why, and perhaps how, I dealt with addiction, as it affected my husband. In addition, I think that information conveyed regarding my friends' lives may even assist readers in recognizing one or more of their loved ones/friends in the personality of one or more of my friends, thus establishing a connection between the reader and my memoir.

In the midst of chaos,
hope, joy, and victory
can still abound.

CHAPTER TWO

THE BROTHER-FIGURE ADDICK

~ Bill Jenkins ~

Every time we ate dinner, Bill always used to say, "From the rooter to the tooter."

Invariably, minutes later, I had to use the bathroom.

At six-foot, four-inches tall, Bill weighed 190 pounds and possessed a washboard stomach. His complexion hinted at smooth, silky caramel candy. His dark brown eyebrows and eyelashes complimented a thin mustache. His teeth bedazzled to pearly white perfection. His looks alone sent most women into the stratosphere.

I met Bill, a sophomore at St. Augustine High School, at the bus stop on our way to school one day. I attended Gregory Junior High and was finishing my last year there before starting high school at Abramson Senior High. When I approached the bus stop, Bill sat there drumming his fingers on his knees and singing one of the Commodores' hottest hits, *Brickhouse*.

Bill gazed at me. "Yes, ma'am, you can sit next to me any time cause *you're a brick house, you're mighty-mighty just lettin' it all hang out.*"

I do have to admit that super cute described my appearance that fateful day. I had donned my favorite outfit because yearbook pictures during homeroom had been scheduled for that day. My favorite colors in those days included all earth tones, such as browns, blacks, mustards, and olive greens, just to name a few. So, I wore a brown, fitted, sleeveless, mid-thigh dress that flared out at the bottom and was decorated with orange, mustard, and brown tulips the size of grapefruits. The colors in the dress brought out my golden-toned thighs.

Bill extended his hand to assist me with sitting down while scooting over to make room for me, showcasing his gentleness. "My name is Bill Jenkins, Angel."

Uncertain as to why he had called me Angel, I assumed that he had used an endearment because many people in New Orleans use endearments such as angel, baby, and sweetie. It wasn't until two years later that I learned that his endearment for me came wrapped in deeper emotions, which I will detail further as I delve into the development of our relationship.

"Uh...hi. My name is Vivian."

"It's a pleasure meeting you. What's your last name?"

"Thomas."

"Angel Thomas, and you're headed where?"

"To school."

"What school do you go to?"

"Gregory Junior High."

"I bet that you're the smartest girl in school. I won't bet on you being the prettiest cause that's a given." Bill opened his backpack and retrieved a notebook and a pen. "Would it be okay if we exchange phone numbers? No way does an angel appears before my eyes and I don't get her contact information."

Bill wrote Angel Thomas on the inside cover of his notebook and waited for me to give him my phone number.

I gave Bill my phone number, and from that day forward, our friendship grew stronger, and regardless of the number of times that I reminded him of my birth name, Vivian Thomas, he continued to call me Angel. He even articulated that he liked my first name, but to him, whenever he thought of me, he felt in his heart that I was Angel.

When Bill called my house, he requested to speak to Angel Thomas. Sometimes the person who answered the phone didn't know who he meant.

After a time or two, my mom, my dad, and my sisters came to know who he was calling for. In the thirty-five years that I knew Bill; I never heard him refer to another person as Angel.

Bill and I became close friends, like brother and sister. When he graduated from high school in May of 1980, two years after we met, his mom threw him a huge graduation party at the Marriott Hotel in downtown New Orleans. Invitees included his entire graduation class and his closest neighborhood friends. After the party, a group of us walked along Canal Street to the River Front, a popular strip of pathway, now referred to as a segment of the Riverwalk, used for walking along the Mississippi River.

Many of our friends thought that our relationship had evolved into an intimate one, but it had not, though that night a commitment to be honest with one another, no matter what, did become the foundation for its longevity.

Bill stared at the moon from the River Front, by which the Mississippi River flows. "You're my angel. I will never lie to you, and I'll always be there for you. I love you with all my soul. I have no sisters or brothers, so you are my sister, my friend, my confidant, and only death will separate us. If I ever find a girlfriend or a wife, she will have to accept our relationship. If she doesn't or can't, then she is not the girl for me. I love you more than I would love a girlfriend and more than I would love a wife. Angel, you have pierced my heart in a spot that has never been pierced before. I can't imagine another piercing of this kind. And I want to thank you."

My mind froze and left me speechless.

When my mind thawed and untied my tongue, I sounded like a shy, 12-year-old girl, "Bill, I feel the same way. Over the last two years, you have been my friend and my champion. On days when I felt lonely or needed you to defend me from a bully and I called you, you made me feel loved and protected. You are my brother, and whoever I end up with will have to accept that, or they will have to move on.

"You have a lot of girls falling at your feet, and not one time did you make me feel unwanted. In fact, a lot of those girls act funny with me because I think that they're jealous of our friendship. But why haven't you made advances toward me? Most guys do."

Bill kissed me on the lips. "Because I love you too much. On the day that I met you, sorrow assailed my life because a week before we met, my mom and dad had announced, without explanation, their intention to divorce, and a couple of days after that, my dad informed me that my mom had been unfaithful and that no matter what he did, he could never please her.

"He called her a black widow because he felt that she had killed every husband she ever had, and he thought that he might be her next victim. My mom was married and divorced four times before she married my dad. All four of her husbands had died from unnatural causes. I didn't know any of this until after my dad and I had this discussion about their impending divorce.

"He invited me to live with him and warned me to remain vigilant when in my mother's care. I didn't quite know what his warning meant because my mom treated me like a king. I couldn't imagine her harming me.

Bill grabbed my hand in earnest. "Sitting on that bench at the bus stop, on the day that I met you, bewilderment had my mind in a hellish state of being. I almost didn't go to school that day. I wanted to disappear, in the hope that my pain would too. I felt alone and scared. And then you appeared. At first, I thought that God had sent me an angel because five minutes before you appeared, I sat mesmerized wishing for an angel to rescue me from this agony because I did not want to be here anymore bearing all this pain. And even though I surrounded myself with so many people, well, girls, I still felt alone. Then you appeared.

Ever since then, I've felt such comfort around you. Sex crosses my mind every time I see you, but I'm afraid to pursue it because I don't want to lose my angel or the relationship that we've built. Now, if we become husband and wife, *I'ma rock yo' world! I'ma send ya' to visit yo' Daddy up in heaven with a note that He gotta send ya' back 'cause I ain't through yet!*" Bill enacted his rendition of Wanda from the Jamie Fox sitcom. He often imitated TV personalities when attempting to make a light-hearted point.

I cracked up. "That's what I love most about you, your ability to transition from the sane to the insane."

In August of 1981, a year and three months after graduating from high school, Bill became the manager of Chess King, a teens and men's retail store, located within the Read Road Plaza Mall, a store at which he had been working since his 11th grade-year of high school. His taste in clothes reminded me of the models featured in men's fashion magazines. Impeccable. As the manager, Bill was paid a salary that afforded him to move into an upscale apartment with amenities such as major appliances, a swimming pool, a spa, and an exercise room, all in a gated community. He purchased a pearl white, fully loaded 1979 Corvette.

We partied every other weekend. With my spare key, I could hang out at his place whenever I wanted. On most days Bill had a stash of marijuana, and he always had alcohol and wine. His place became my haven.

For the next three years Bill and I dated other people, including one another's friends, but as we had promised, they had to accept our friendship, or we sent them on their way. We had an extraordinary relationship.

I think that my pregnancy disappointed Bill, but he offered his support by giving me money and his heart-felt friendship, particularly since my relationship with Eric consistently wavered somewhere between tepid and frosty. I could depend on Bill to be the constant and strong pillar that I needed. In November of 1986, five years after Erika's birth, Bill married Betty, one of his co-workers, and a month later, they welcomed a son, whom they named Bill Jr.

In January of 1987, a month following the birth of Bill Jr., Bill was promoted to Regional Manager with Chess King. He managed twenty stores in ten states. He worked together with six different buyers. On average, Bill's job required that he work out of town for at least five months out of the year.

At first, Bill, being away for prolonged periods of time, did not present any issues for him and Betty, but after a couple of years, the frequency of Bill's out-of-town trips affected their relationship negatively. Between his new job, his baby son, and his wife, Bill endured excruciating pressure. In coping with this pressure, Bill decreased his appetite for marijuana as his appetite for cocaine increased. He called me from time to time to release steam and to secure some semblance of peace.

Betty labored with constant agony over missing Bill, feelings of loneliness, coping as a single parent most of the time, and desiring more of a local relationship. Yet, her inability to produce the income that Bill generated left her trapped in a marriage that burdened them both. She refused to live without the sizable income that Bill earned, which made certain that she could continue to benefit from all of the comforts that she had become so accustomed to. So, she remained married to Bill, but she was unfaithful. Bill closed his eyes to her unfaithfulness, while all of the signs of infidelity (silent phone calls, unnecessary trips to the store, increased partying with girlfriends, lack of interest in sex) bombarded him upon each return home.

Though Bill's heart ached, I hated to say I told you so, so I didn't. But I had never seen her as the woman for him, and as his closet friend, I communicated that to him. He thought otherwise. In terms of intellect and maturity, the jury was still out, but the strength of their relationship had always relied on their physical attraction to one another. But honestly, that was not enough to sustain a marriage.

Bill loved his job. It expanded his horizons by connecting him to various parts of the world. He even met and worked with famous designers and, on occasion, well-known celebrities. It thrilled my heart to know that he had found his dream job. Our friendship meant so much to both of us. Quite often I reminisced about the many times that he had come to my defense.

Once, he showed up to my house with a gun, screaming, "Where that nigga at? I'ma kill his punk ass!"

This kind of anger took Bill outside of his normal character, and in our culture referring to another person as a nigger was not offensive; similar to how the way many rappers use the word. In fact, I've heard it used in so many ways that the Black people I know aren't offended when other Blacks use it.

Bill's anger arose when a mutual friend informed him that a guy I was dating, Eli Porche, had hit me. I didn't want Bill to go to jail because of that, so I refused to inform him of Eli's whereabouts. Besides, I had inflicted enough pain on Eli when I hit him in the face with one of those old-time rotary phones. Thinking back on Bill coming to my defense against Eli, it dawned on me that, in my subconscious, my relationship with Eli factored into my decision to move to San Jose.

I had always been a fighter. Fighting didn't scare me, girls, boys, it didn't matter to me. A fight was a fight. Every morning when I was 7 or 8 years old, my aunt Sis, my daddy's sister, walked my oldest sister and me to school through the Magnolia Projects, a low-income housing community, which was known for violence. I'm not sure why my mom enrolled us in that school because we didn't live within the projects. I'm guessing that it had an outstanding academic program.

But during those walks, my aunt always instructed us to knock the hell out of anyone who picked on us. And if they possessed a stature grander than ours, we were to pick up an object to use as a weapon and whoop their behinds. In fact, if I thought that an adversary intended to hit me, her advice was always, to hit them first because sometimes the first lick is the last. Though this was in stark contrast to what my mom taught us, for some reason, this stuck with me.

After living in San Jose for more than four years, on one cool and breezy Friday morning in the spring of 1992, out of the blue, Bill called to tell me that he would be in San Francisco on business that evening and wanted to see me while he was in town. My heart instantly filled with astonishment and anticipation at the prospect of seeing my dear brother and friend. After work, I drove to San Francisco International Airport to pick him up.

What a reunion! We ate dinner at Fisherman's Wharf, on the northern waterfront of the San Francisco Bay, one of the city's busiest tourist areas. We drove all around San Francisco before entering into San Jose to spend the weekend at my place. On that Sunday morning, Bill and I discussed his departure from San Jose. He had taken a one-week vacation so that we could spend the week together.

I thought it strange that he had planned to stay for a week without giving me any advance notice to ensure that I could take a week, or at least a few days, off of work.

"Bill, why didn't you call me a week ago? I could have taken time off from work." I stirred the pot of grits boiling.

"I didn't know until two days ago. I meant to call you, but I kept forgetting due to all of the last-minute requests from my clients. But I thought that I mentioned it when I called on Friday morning that I wanted to spend the week with you."

"No, you didn't. You only mentioned that you would be in San Francisco on business on Friday evening and that you wanted to see me. When are you going home?" I waited for his response not knowing what to expect.

"I'm not sure about going home to New Orleans."

"What? What do you mean?"

"Well, you know that my marriage is over, and I'm not feeling New Orleans anymore."

"Yeah, I know that y'all broke up. But not living in New Orleans, are you serious? You're contemplating not living in New Orleans?"

Bill dropped the unexpected. "Well, yeah, but it's more than that. I need my Angel. I didn't realize how my relationship with Betty would never work until after we married. I thought that it would grow to be like my relationship with you, but it didn't. I felt so alone and disconnected from her. Why do you think that I called you so much? I couldn't talk to her the way that we talked, which is why I think she felt like I loved you more than I loved her. I tried to explain to her that I loved you differently, not more. But she disagreed and could not mentally process the nature of our relationship.

"With you I felt a peace and a calmness that I couldn't feel with her. I tried, but I didn't feel it. For a while, it felt better when I stayed on the road. At home, I didn't feel better unless I drank and smoked crack. Whatever it took to escape the internal sentiments that oppressed me, though I am disappointed in myself for my disregard for how our situation impacted her, which caused her to lose faith in me and our relationship, so she left. And her leaving produced such a pleasing relief that it felt like I had exhaled, for the first time, after holding my breath throughout the entire length of our marriage. Astounding relieved. We would no longer hurt each other. My deepest regret is that I would no longer be in my son's life the way that I wanted to and that another man would end up raising him."

"I'm so sorry to hear about the unhappiness that you experienced. Since I've been in San Jose, work and raising Erika has been my primary focus. Last month I enrolled in the University of San Francisco to complete my degree. In eighteen months, I'll have my bachelor's degree in Organizational Behavior.

"As for my romantic life, it's as dead as a doorknob, and I've been content with that because I don't like bringing strange men around Erika. But there are days when I'm lonely. And I've thought of you often since I've been here."

"That's what's up! You're missing me, and I'm missing you! "Where is Erika now?" Bill's demeanor brightened considerably.

"She's spending the summer with my mom. That's why I enrolled in school now. It gives me a chance to get used to studying while working a full-time job so that when she returns, I'll be able to take care of her without the newness of going to school."

Bill and I stared at one another for a minute, though it felt like an hour.

His gaze pierced my soul as he whispered, "I missed you. I missed us and our mutual closeness. Between my job, my marriage, and the problems that I've been having with my mom and dad, I am exhausted and about ready to detonate. I often wonder whether if life hadn't separated us, and we had pursued an intimate relationship, would my life be any different? Would I be the person I used to be?"

I could feel the sadness in Bill's heart. "What do you mean by 'the person you used to be'?"

"Let's go for a walk, and I'll tell you all about it."

CHAPTER THREE

THE FUNNIEST ADDICK I KNOW
~ Ricky Flores ~

Ricky Flores, a name known only to those with whom Ricky conducted official business or familiar with close family members. Most people call him Chico. To know his true name meant that he classified you as a member of the family or an adopted family member. To him, individual people created their own family, not birthright, and the title *friend* indicated that you were an acquaintance, but not close enough for him to label you as a family member. His relationship with you placed you as a business-related person, an acquaintance, or a family member.

Chico, an incredibly attractive teenager with dark chocolate, creamy, smooth skin, had charisma to spare. The moon-shaped curly locks that laid flat against his temple, which he pulled back into a ponytail, flowed down to the bottom of his neck like a river of oil. His charcoal black eyebrows and eyelashes reminded me of a child's tracing of the edges of a picture in a coloring book. Milk chocolate pupils glittered when he smiled, and his marble white teeth stood as straight as soldiers at attention. He didn't wear a mustache or a beard.

Born in the Dominican Republic, at the age of 16, he and his family moved to New Orleans. Chico spoke with a thick Dominican Spanish accent. I remember when he explained his perspective of a friend to me.

Chico's words spoken in English came out fast and choppy with an over-use of English slang. "Da only friend I have is Jesus 'cause He's da only one dat ever laid His life down for mines. Can you think of anotha' friend dat did dat for you? I didn't thank you could, and if you eva' find one, he is indeed a friend."

Chico had two older brothers and four younger sisters. He described his father as a businessman and his mother as a housewife. Chico never talked about his immediate family, so I never knew much about them.

From all indications, Chico's father's success in his profession spoke volumes. He and his family traveled across the country and to other countries every summer and during some school breaks. His family lavished in the best living that money could buy.

Chico lived in opulence and luxury. Their house sat on Lake Pontchartrain, a secluded area in New Orleans East, directly on the lakefront with a panoramic view of the downtown skyline and Lake Pontchartrain from two balconies. The kitchen and living rooms had open areas built for entertainment. Situated on navigable water, the house had a private boat slip and a clubhouse, a sauna, and a pool. From the street, at the end of their driveway, a bunch of trees, shrubs, and other landscaping kept their house hidden from the public.

Chico and I met at a house party in July of 1984, to which my friend Lylah Bastion invited me. Spence, with an unknown last name, and Lylah's friend, threw a party at his brother's house for reasons unknown to me. Lylah invited me, and because I liked partying, I accepted her invitation.

When I met Chico, Lylah had left me sitting by the pool, my feet in the warm water, while she ventured off with Spence to another section of the house. I didn't discover her whereabouts until after the party.

Chico walked up behind me. "Excuze me."

Man, what a handsome guy. "Yes."

"I hate to dizturb ya, but it appears ya having too much fun alone, and around hea' dat can't be. So, I've been sent to join in on some of da fun, if ya don't mine."

"And if I do mind?"

"Den I won't mine for ya." He dazzled me with that dazzling smile.

"Well, in that case, I better not mind.

"Yeah, ya right, ya betta' not. Ya don't want me mining ya bizness. 'Cause for sho', I can mine otha folks' bizness."

Chico sat down next to me and dangled his feet in the water. "My name's Chico."

"I'm Vivian."

We talked for the rest of the party. His personality was as pleasant and funny as it could be. I couldn't imagine laughing any harder, other than at a professional comedian's jokes, than I laughed with Chico. His attempt at speaking in English caused him to have a deep but cute accent, which may have contributed to him being so funny.

By the end of the party, Chico and I had swapped numbers, drank at least three or four long island ice teas, smoked two or three joints, danced, swam in our clothes, and talked and joked as if we had known one another all of our lives. I had to hand it to him, having him around, I did not have fun alone. He made that party one of the best parties that I have ever been to.

A couple of days later, Chico called at 5:30 p.m. "Hey, what ya doin'? Ya feel like company?"

"Sure." I gave him my address and directions to my house.

He lived twenty minutes away, but it took him forty-five minutes to ring my doorbell. I opened the door.

Chico stood there with a bottle of wine tucked under his left arm, a box of food that had an aroma that weakened my knees in his left hand, CDs in his right hand, and a huge grin on his face. "Special delivery."

"What's in the box?"

"Didn't ya know that I bring a party wit' me everywhere I go?"

"Boy, you are too funny!" He entered the house.

"Ya 'bout the fiftieth person who told me dat, and dat's just today. Ump, dat shit must be truth. Well, my crazy ass bought ya some catfish, shrimp, oysters, and French fries. I know ya like seafood 'cause I ain't met a single person in New Orleens dat don't like seafood and Aaron Neville."

I laughed and imitated his accent. "You ain't lying."

"I might be crazy, but I don't lie."

I led Chico to the kitchen, retrieved plates and glasses for the food and drinks, ran upstairs and grabbed the CD player, then led him to the backyard patio where I set the plates, the food, the drinks, and the CD player. We ate and listened to the CDs that he had brought with him. I didn't have to tell him to make himself comfortable because he did that on his own.

As we sat in the backyard, enjoying ourselves, one of my sisters and Erika spied on us, curious about Chico and hoping to quench their thirst for additional intel. I introduced Chico to both of them. He offered them food and, of course, they didn't refuse.

It wasn't long before my dad's inquiring mind got the best of him because he too appeared in the backyard, so I introduced him to Chico, and Chico offered him some food along with a glass of wine. Of course, my dad accepted.

Chico and I sat in the backyard until 2:00 in the morning learning about each other's past, our desires, and and our hopes for the future. He recalled his move to New Orleans, without disclosing too many details about why his family had moved to my fair city.

"My dad moved us hea' because he always wanted to live in New Orleens. He doesn't like my mom workin' outside of the home. He prefers tha' she be a homemaka'."

"Is that what she wants?"

"I guess." He didn't say it, but his body language shifted, and without his saying a word, it became clear that he wasn't comfortable with this line of questioning or the conversation itself.

So, I switched up the discourse. "So, how do you know Spence?"

"My dad worked wit' Charles, Spence's brotha'."

"Spence's brother, oh, the guy who owns the house where the party was?"

"Yeah."

It was time for me to satisfy my own curiosity. "Who does your dad work for?"

"He has his own business, but he has business partnus' who work wit' him."

"Do you work with your dad too?"

"Naw, I prefa' to do my own bizness. I work wit' my hands. I like takin' apart, fixin' and buildin' stuff."

"Wow, did you take woodshop in high school?"

"Yeah. And I also finis' two trades at Delgado, carpentry and mechanics. If I finished da mechanics program, my dad promised to buy me a classic ca' to fix up, and when I'm done fixin' it up, it could be wort' a bundle of money. So, I finis' da program, and he bought me a 1945 Excaliba'. I fix'd it up, and it is cleen. I don't drive it every day. I'm preservin' it and lettin' it grow in value."

I sat straight up. "Delgado? I'm in Delgado too. I'm taking accounting at night."

"Is dat right? I bet chu' smart as a whip. I've also enrolled in air conditionin' and refrig'ration. And I've been thinkin' about becomin' an electrician once I'm finis'. I like dat kind of stuff. And I like creatin' all kinds of stuff."

"So do you have customers that you work for?"

"Yeah. Right now, I work for a furniture sto' restorin' furniture. My mom shoulda' named me Jack 'cause I'm a jack of all trades." His smile bedazzled again.

"Well, Jack, are you master of any?"

"Hell, yeah. Wit' all my trades, I'm a master in makin' money."

We both laughed.

Chico and I had a wonderful time that night. And I discovered that we both loved Aaron Neville. Chico and I both knew the words to every one of Aaron's songs. I also found out that he had turned 22 years old in the same month that I turned 21. Two May babies who had had birthdays two months before meeting.

Over the next four years, Chico and I became close friends. He called me from time to time to vent about his dad or mom wanting to control his life and not affording him an opportunity to live his own life. His primary complaint was that they interfered whenever he wanted to make his own decisions, and this boiled his blood the most. One time he called so mad that he ranted on about not wanting the same lifestyle as his dad, always peering over his shoulder for danger or having unwarranted suspicions about acquaintances and uprooting the family, making them start all over building relationships and familiarities in new places. He even vented about how he didn't want a woman like his mom, one without a voice.

One time, Chico tried his best to swallow his tears. "I like New Orleans, and I have no plans to leave any time soon."

Totally baffled, I thought to myself, what is all of this about. Since I didn't have a clue, I listened until he ended the phone call.

Another time he showed up at my house, and we sat in his car as he bawled.

"I'm sick of dis' shit!" Chico scrunched up his face.

"What shit?"

"I dunno, I'm jus' tired of it all!"

"Tired of what shit? Chico, what's going on?"

He shook his head. "I dunno. I dunno."

I didn't get it. He had me in a state of confusion. Questioning him didn't help because he released no explanation or clarity.

What a frustrating night for both of us. I didn't know what had him in such a frenzy. I knew clearly that he carried within himself a tremendous amount of pressure. As we sat in the car, he rambled on and even cried. I sat there and listened. What else could I do?

Two days later, Chico called and acted as if two days ago had never happened. He flaunted his normal, happy, funny self without a hint of frustration, anger, or sadness. He didn't even mention the episode, but I did.

"So, umm, how are you?" I rubbed my hands together.

"Oh, I'm good. Thanks for hearin' me out the otha' day. I appre'ciate ya. I can't thank ya enough."

"No problem. That's what friends are for. What was that all about?"

"Ahhh, nothin'. I'm good. Jus' sometimes I be trippin'. No worries."

I sensed enough apprehension in his voice to know that he didn't want to elaborate any further, so I dropped the subject, but he did thank me two or three additional times for being there for him with a listening ear.

I recall incidents of this nature occurring five or six more times, and after every time, he always acted as if the incident hadn't occurred, yet he was always apologetic and thankful for my support. After the third or fourth time that this happened, I stopped wondering about the underlying cause of the episode and focused on being the support that he needed.

For the most part, in every phone conversation and in every in-person engagement, he managed to be the life of the party and one of the most giving people I had ever met. Chico had a humongous heart and was always willing to help. He didn't trust most people, but if someone ever won his trust, his heart would be all theirs. Somehow, I won his trust, my family won his trust, and from that moment he adopted us as his family.

We invited him to all of our family functions, and he showed up ready to party. And he invited my family and me to his family's functions, and a few though they were, and never held at his house, we attended to show our support. When Chico graduated from Delgado's air conditioning and refrigeration program, a couple of years after our meeting, sometime in 1986, his family celebrated the occasion by renting out a ballroom, the presidential suite, and one floor of rooms at the New Orleans Sheraton Hotel for family and close friends. Food and drink were served, seemingly without end. Though Chico did not see himself as privileged, events such as this proved that he was indeed privileged.

As close as Chico and I were, I didn't spend a lot of time around his family outside of family functions. Whenever I visited him at his house, his mom and dad always greeted me cordially and pleasantly, but I always had this feeling that accepting me kept peace between Chico and them. I can't pinpoint any particular incident or words spoken that brought on such feelings or that explained why our friendship would keep peace between them other than perhaps a gut feeling or intuition.

By the time that I left New Orleans in 1988, Chico was my second closest male friend and one of the funniest guys I have ever known. I could always count on him to pick my spirits up regardless of the kind of day I experienced. His hands proved to be his secret jewels. That man could fix whatever gadget, machine, or whatnot that broke. He reminded me of my cousin Reg, who was also a mechanic. They embraced the same perspectives on assembling products. They both felt that companies (which they both referred to as *the people*) don't make assembling products hard. If something is hard to assemble, the assembler is constructing it wrong.

Quite often I find myself remembering their perspectives, which always leads me to re-evaluate how I'm doing what I'm doing and then to use a different approach, if necessary. And with a different approach, in no time, the product invariably works as the manufacturer intended it to work.

I considered Chico to be a genius in his own way. He had a heart that stretched beyond the moon, though, he could piss me off, and I mean to the highest level of pissivity, a word that should be in Webster's Dictionary but is not. But no way in hell could I stay there. I have no idea how many times he pissed me off to the point where I didn't want to deal with him ever again, but after a few days, I couldn't stay mad at him, even when I tried. And only the Lord knows how many times over the years I have tried.

CHAPTER FOUR

THE GENEROSITY OF AN ADDICK

~ Lylah Bastion ~

Lylah Bastion, my girl, and some kind of lady. With her long, thin, narrow face, most people did not consider her to be the prettiest girl on the block. Her body might have reminded one of a number 2 pencil. If I had to guess, I would say that she weighed all of 105 pounds soaking wet, though she stood at six feet, three-inches tall.

She had the skin tone of an Indian. In fact, most people considered her nationality to be Indian, but her family's origins were Puerto Rican and African American, though she spoke only English. Her mom's pale skin and her dad's raisin-toned skin produced her chestnut skin, her complexion a warm brown with hints of redness. Her pitch-black hair poured down her neck and spread across her back like a silk drape. And the dimple in her chin was a clue as to why so many people thought her to be Indian.

At times Lylah could be insecure about herself, and my guest as to why was because of her chipped front tooth, though this was mostly unnoticeable due to the way that her thin lips moved when she talked. But because she knew that the chipped tooth existed, she thought that it stuck out like a sore thumb.

Lylah had a cool, calm, and collected type of personality. Lylah did not walk, rather she strolled with long, slow-paced strides, like a cat, quiet, with calculated motion. And if cornered or trapped, she scratched herself free. She demanded respect and fought like a prize fighter to defend her pride. She never hesitated to correct anyone who disrespected her with names like "bitch" or "whore," making it clear that she did not tolerate that — and it enraged her. In fact, her exact words to me proclaimed, *Bitches walk on four legs, and whores keep their legs spread, and the last time I checked, I did not do neither.* She pronounced neither with a long I.

Her family moved from Manhattan, New York, in 1978, during her ninth-grade year of high school. I met Lylah when I started school at Abramson Senior High School in the fall of 1979. Because I finished my ninth grade year at Gregory Jr. High, we were two sophomores eager to connect with a classmate who held similar perspectives on friendship. Lylah was more of an introvert than an extrovert. We both did not like confusion, creating animosity with or among others, we did not spread rumors, and neither of us minded other people's business. Most girls that I knew did not fit within the parameters of our views on friendship, so Lylah, one or two other girls, and I hung together. Lylah did not talk much. She communicated through gestures and body language, often through her eyes. I found it intriguing, yet weird, but I accepted her for her.

Lylah and Spence dated in secret. She didn't talk excessively about him or her feelings for him the way that most girls talked about their boyfriends. If I had not known her, I would have thought that she didn't trust me to know more about him. But I am certain that that's not how she felt. That was just Lylah regarding her business.

Lylah didn't have a fussy personality, but when provoked to anger, I never had to wonder what she thought or how she felt. She never threw out idle threats. She called them promises. When she said to stop or didn't want you in her face, she meant it.

Some of the jealous girls in school, who took her quietness for weakness, learned the hard way that Lylah didn't initiate altercations, but if you brought one to her, and she verbalized that she would kick your behind, you could count on her doing just that. After laying out the warning, *I don't mind wiping you bitches all over this parking lot*, she dragged her opponent across the parking lot, as promised.

The year that we graduated, 1981, Lylah's parents had given her an ultimatum. She either had to go to college or find a job. She chose to find a job. After applying at numerous places and working two different jobs and not liking either the job or the people there, Lylah accepted an offer that her parents made for her to work for the family business.

Her parents owned and operated their own home interior decorating company that they called Bastion's Designs. At first, she didn't like it, but she had to work there or hit the pavement seeking work elsewhere. She decided that working for her parents was easier than interviewing with other companies.

After working for her parents for six or seven months, Lylah gained confidence in learning and performing the job, and her parents paid her a salary commensurate with other design companies' entry level new hires. She didn't have bills to pay, so she spent the majority of her money on whatever she desired. She still lived with her parents, so they covered her housing, utilities, food, and medical expenses.

After a year or so of working for her parents, Lylah realized that she loved the job and decided to present two or three of her own designs to her parents. Her parents voiced their amazement at Lylah's natural talent for designing. Her mom encouraged her to go to design school to hone her talent, but Lylah didn't want to go to school, which disappointed her mom. But her mom hoped and prayed that one day Lylah would go to design school.

The closeness that Lylah and I valued, both in high school and after we developed into young women, resulted from our similarities in that she never over-talked, and like me, she refused to be a pushover. I could confide in her, and I knew that my business would be safe with her.

Over the next five years, I took part in lots of personal moments with her. Lylah never criticized or ridiculed me. If I solicited her opinion or advice, she gave it to me with no expectation that I would use it. She never bragged or reveled in *I told you so* when she was right on her predictions. If her warning proved correct, she acknowledged it with a nod and moved on. If the outcome of her prediction brought sorrow or any kind of pain, she comforted me and offered encouragement and/or assistance. She had so much compassion and was never hesitant about showing it in her own quiet way.

Performing acts of kindness towards others came as first nature to Lylah, including acts of kindness towards animals. She never talked about it before or afterwards. She simply acted.

I recall Lylah once stopping the car, as we were on our way to run the obstacle course at the University of New Orleans, and giving a wounded dog a can of Vienna sausages, which she pulled right out of her purse, and a drink of water from a bottle of water that she had in her car. While the dog devoured the Vienna sausages, she retrieved an old towel from the trunk of her car and wrapped the dog in the towel. Lylah took the dog to an animal shelter and wrote a $100.00 check for the care of the dog. Lylah was 23 years old, and made decent money, so writing a check for $100.00 didn't phase her one bit. She was a giver, and whenever the need to give presented itself, she gave.

When we returned to the car, she grimaced and mumbled, "I hope that he's okay."

I sat in awe of her kindness.

Lylah's personal relationship with her parents and her two brothers seemed estranged. Whenever I witnessed the interaction between her and her family, they acted more cordially toward each other rather than fond of one another. I never witnessed a close moment between any of them. It always felt like a dress rehearsal, like they were going through the motions, but without any emotion. There didn't appear to be any genuine affection between them. Even their merriment seemed muffled.

One day when riding in her car, I opened a conversation about her relationship with her parents. "Are you and your parents tight?"

"We're cool."

"What about you and your brothers?"

"They're all right most times. Though sometimes they get on my nerves and are aggravating. Other than that, they're cool."

"So, why you don't bring them to chill with us from time to time when we're hanging out at the lake?"

"Well, Spikey is 16, and though Breeze is a year younger than me, he has his own world going on." Lylah sounded nonchalant about them hanging with us.

"What do you mean he has his own world going on?"

"You know, he's doing Breeze, and I'm doing Lylah. Besides, he knows the place, and if he shows up, he shows up."

I pushed for answers. "Well, does he have a girlfriend?

"Girl, please. I don't do his business. All I know is that he knows girls, and he has friends. Why?"

"Because he seems like he would be fun to hang out with, that's why. Besides, he's fine as heck!"

"No, you did not just call my brother fine!" Lylah slammed on the brakes.

"Yes, I did, but that's where that ends because I'm not into doing my girlfriends' relatives. That usually leads to trouble. But in case you didn't know, your brother is gorgeous."

"If you think so." Lylah blasted the radio.

Up until I moved to San Jose in 1988, Lylah and I attended so many house parties that I lost count. Impromptu gatherings and backroom parties are what we called them back then. These get-togethers became parties when three or four people assembled in a backroom of someone's house or a hole in the wall spot which is typically a bar, club, or venue to indulge in and experience a moment of bliss. Smoking a joint and drinking a glass of wine or a beer always preceded the mirror, on which the cocaine lay waiting for its next user, that eventually made it around the room. And at the moment of the most anticipated pleasure, a joint laced with cocaine ushered the high to the next dimension of pure delight. And then to top it all off, a swig of the person's desired thirst-quenching libation cranked the high up even more.

31

As I think back on those days, I wonder what on earth possessed me to cause such harm to myself, in the name of fun, which could have led to a premature death or a quality-of-life changing moment that I would have regretted for the rest of my life. I can imagine God thinking to Himself, *My child, what is she doing? Trying to meet me before I'm ready? I better keep my hand on her.*

In 1983, Lylah received private lessons in home and fashion design from friends of her parents. These friends worked directly with professionally known designers. While taking these lessons, Lylah's mom saw her prayers answered, Lylah enrolled in the University of New Orleans (UNO) and majored in Business Administration. Lylah's home and fashion design lessons lasted about a year and a half. Lylah's mom mentioned, in my presence, at least three or four times how grateful and overjoyed she felt that her friends agreed to work with Lylah because they too witnessed Lylah's natural fashion design talent and that with their tutelage she could soar to the top of the home and fashion design industry. Lylah graduated, with honors, from UNO in May of 1988.

With her raw talent and her education, Lylah rose in prominence in her field and landed a job in Los Angeles, California, with a top fashion design firm. The level of pressure which Lylah did not even know existed, due to the fierceness of the competition, overwhelmed her. Though successful in her career, she felt that the cost of that success outweighed the benefits, so she quit the firm after almost five years, returned to New Orleans, and joined her parents as a business partner instead of an employee.

As a new business partner, Lylah brought a level of expertise that she incorporated into the Bastion's Designs brand creating an entire new line and style of home designs, and with her parents' reputation, the family business prospered. Lylah made more money than she ever dreamed that she could make.

After returning to New Orleans, Lylah and Spence rekindled the old flame between them, but this time, she preferred that her friends and family be aware of her relationship with Spence. By this time, I had already moved to San Jose.

She called me to inform me that she had returned to New Orleans. "Hey girl! How's it going?"

"I'm good, what's new with you."

"Well, quite a bit. I've left Los Angeles, and I'm back home now. And Spence and I are dating. I invited him to dinner with the family, and all seems good."

"Wow! That's great. I'm so glad to hear that you have moved back home. Next time I'm in town, I'll be sure to visit you. And great news about you and Spence."

After that, I ensured that every trip home included visiting Lylah and spending at least a day or two with her. Each time that I popped in, she seemed happy and content, though I did notice a slight personality shift in that the introvert that I had always encountered in the past no longer existed. I guess that living in Los Angeles, in the business world, lured her out of her shell, and this was a joy for me to see. It added a delicious flavor to her that enlarged her presence.

Her compassion for others had changed. It appeared heightened and more pronounced. Lylah's involvement in fundraisers for charities and causes grew to the point that I could not name them all: churches, Girl Scouts, Boy Scouts, battered women, homes for the homeless, cancer, and feeding the hungry. You name it, she had a donation going toward it.

One time when I visited her, I witnessed her buying cars for two single parents, who she saw with their kids as they waited for the bus to pick the kids up to take them to daycare and the parents to their jobs.

The day that Lylah gave the cars to those two ladies amazed me. She pulled up slightly past the bus stop where the two ladies sat, waiting on the bus. She cut the car off and instructed me to come with her. When she approached the bus stop she smiled and introduced herself.

"Hi, my name is Lylah."

"Hi!" the ladies harmonized.

"I know you don't know me, but I have watched the two of you sit at this bus stop with your children for years dreaming that one day I could help you all obtain a car so that you wouldn't have to endure the hassle of catching the bus. Well, ladies, today is the day that I make my dream a reality."

Lylah pulled from her purse two sets of keys and four business cards and handed each lady a set of keys and two business cards.

"Ladies, these are the keys to the cars I have purchased for each of you. This is my business card, and this is the business card of the dealership I would like you to meet me at to complete the transaction for you to receive your car."

The ladies' facial expressions could not hide the bewilderment they felt. One lady's jaw dropped as she covered her face in disbelief while the other lady jumped to her feet overjoyed, yet in awe.

"Please call me later today or tomorrow before 7:00 pm. If you would like, I can pick you up or you can meet me at the dealership; the address is on the card. Either option will work for me."

The ladies thanked Lylah and said they would call her after they return home from work that same day. Lylah gave them both a hug and left. After pulling away from the bus stop, Lylah realized she never even asked the ladies their names.

After witnessing her generosity towards those ladies, my heart simply erupted. "Lylah, you are the most generous person I know. It's mind-blowing that you bought cars for those ladies."

"Well, I watched those ladies every morning year after year, on my way to work, and I couldn't go another day without helping them. Did you see the joy on their faces? Priceless!"

"Well, I'm astonished! You are so amazing, and I will never forget this moment."

I'm sure that those ladies were oblivious to what Lylah did for them. Lylah's generosity delivered, in volumes, the very nature of Lylah. She knew how to be Lylah and never regretted it, even if people didn't realize or appreciate her generosity. And that's what I loved the most about Lylah.

CHAPTER FIVE

REMEMBERING THE GOODNESS

Bill's visit to San Jose in the spring of 1992 landed us walking in the park talking about his life after I left New Orleans and conversing about the many occasions that we had spoken over the phone. At times, I sensed hesitancy in his voice as he tried to explain his situation, and I felt the sadness and hurt as it seeped out through each breath that he took.

Bill finally took the plunge. "My mom lied to me, and my dad isn't my real dad."

"What? Are you serious?"

"Yes, apparently, she had an affair and got pregnant by the guy. That shit really hurt my dad, but he loved her and wanted to raise her baby as his own. They agreed to keep it between the two of them. I found out about a year ago when I needed blood after being shot at a club in New York.

"What! Shot! What the hell! When?"

"Yeah, some fool shot me over some bull-crap."

"What kind of bull-crap?" My face paled in panic.

"Umm, it's nothing, that nigga was tripping."

"Now you're lying. What happened?"

Bill dropped his head. "A deal gone wrong, that's all."

"Like hell that's all. What happened?"

"Can we drop it? It's water under the bridge, and I don't want to talk about it."

"Umm, no! You know what...okay...fine." I didn't push any further because I knew that he didn't want to talk about it, so I let it go, at least for the time being.

As we walked, my mind raced, and concentration became more and more difficult with every step that we took. Bill's vagueness bothered me. We had always talked straight to one another. In fact, we had promised complete honesty. *What is he hiding from me?*

As we approached one of the benches in the park, we stopped, sat down, and took in the beauty of the park. Every glance soothed the eye, it was so breathtaking. The trees were manicured to such perfection as to suggest a splendid scenery in a portrait. Flowers blossomed in yellow, orange, and white so bright that they could have been mistaken for artificial blooms. The birds flew around without care in the world. And the sky was simply exquisite as it showcased its white, fluffy clouds. My thoughts drifted between the clouds, the birds, the splendor of the flowers, and Bill's evasiveness.

"Are you listening to me?" Bill interrupted my thoughts.

"Huh?"

"You're not listening to me. What are you thinking?"

"I'm trying to figure out what's going on with you."

"What do you mean?"

I laid my cards on the table. "Bill, you're beating around the bush. I've known you forever, and I know when you're not being upfront with me. It's as if you're purposely being evasive because you don't know how to divulge what's going on with you. And it's messing with my mind because that's not who we are. Whatever it is, you need to tell me. Remember, we promised that we would always be honest with one another. So, spill it."

"Okay. Um, I'm in a bit of a jam, and I don't know what I'm going to do." Bill buried his face in his hands.

"Talk to me, Bill."

He raised his head. "I can't return to work. When I flew in this morning, as regional manager, I received a fax informing me that all employees employed by or located at the San Francisco store location must participate in a random drug test on Saturday, which is today, or upon the first day of their return after their scheduled day off. I doubt that I can pass a drug test. If I don't pass, I'll lose my job. I took emergency leave and can't return until I'm sure that I can pass a drug test.

"My boss thinks that I flew home because my mom has been hospitalized, and her status is uncertain. After one of my subordinates dropped me off at the airport, I called you. A typical random drug test for any given location lasts about a week before moving on to the next location, but in a different region. I figured that I would stay a week with you and then go home. After being home for about a week, I would check with my boss to see if I'm still needed in San Francisco or should I remain in New Orleans or proceed to another location in my region. And from there, I would dispatch to wherever he indicated."

"Why in the hell did you feel that you had to lie to me about that?"

"I felt embarrassed, and I didn't know how you would react."

"Why would you feel embarrassed? I know that you do drugs, so what are you not telling me?" Now, my outrage was gaining steam.

"Well, it's not the first time that I have skipped out on a drug test. I tested dirty a couple of times."

"Did anyone make you enroll in any kind of program?"

"No, those programs are only for our drivers, those who have a Commercial Driver's License. My job doesn't require a CDL, so I'm not eligible for any of the programs."

"Boy, you know damn well that I would help, but it sounds like you're in a little deep, seeing as how you're on the verge of losing your job. Do you think that you should seek help through a drug intervention program?"

"I think that I'm good there, but I do need to lay off of using, but sometimes it's hard because the pressures of life, the job, the ex, and all of the other bull-crap wears on me more than you can imagine."

I could see the relief on his face. The corners of his mouth curved upward, and that familiar smile illuminated a peaceful release from his worries. As we sat in the park for the rest of the evening, we reminisced about the old days, wondering what and where our mutual friends' lives had led them.

What an amazing feeling having my brother and friend visit me. Being together made us both feel like the teenagers we used to be ten to fifteen years ago.

Bill jumped up and pointed to a tree thirty yards away. "I bet that I can beat you running to that tree."

"I bet that you can't."

Bill and I took off running. We ran with every bit of energy that we could muster up. I beat him to the tree by three steps. We both fell to the ground huffing and puffing.

I entered my work cubicle at 7:00 sharp on Monday morning, with the hope that my boss would agree to me leaving early and approve me to be off on Tuesday, Thursday, and Friday. I didn't ask for Wednesday off because that was a mandatory meeting day, and I didn't think that she would grant the time off, but to my surprise, after explaining my situation to her, she not only gave me the days that I requested, but due to the circumstances and my stellar work ethic, she suggested that I take Wednesday off as well so that I would have the rest of the week to spend with my unexpected guest. What an amazing boss!

I climbed the stairs of my apartment complex at 4:45 p.m. and as I approached the stoop of the stairway, I found the door of my apartment wide open and Bill sitting in the living room with a man I had never seen before. My presence startled Bill.

"Hey, what are you doing home so early?"

"Trying to figure out who this stranger is sitting in my house."

"Oh, he's a friend. His name is Charles."

My open mouth betrayed my shock. "And he's in my house? Umm, Charles, I don't mean to be rude, but I don't know you, and I don't like people I don't know in my house. So, I'm gonna need you to leave."

"No problem, ma'am." Gazing over to Bill, "I'll catch up with you later man."

Bill stepped outside with Charles. I closed the door and proceeded to my bedroom to change my clothes. Upon strolling into the living room, I found Bill on the sofa, hanging his head, his eyes drooping, reminding me of a lost puppy.

I plopped down next to him. "Bill? What's going on with you? You actually brought a stranger into my house where my daughter and I live — that's unacceptable. What the hell? I know that you know that bringing a stranger into my house is beyond over the top."

"I know, and I am so sorry. Sometimes, I don't think. I don't know what happens to me. I guess that my bull-crap makes me irrational. Please forgive me, Angel. You know that I would never want to bring harm to you and Erika. I would kill myself if I did. You are my closest friend, even closer than my ex-wife, and always have been. Please, Angel, forgive me. Don't be mad at me."

His apology couldn't have been more genuine. His face revealed a pain that he could not put into words, and I could not begin to grasp. What weighed so heavy on Bill? And why couldn't he tell me about it?

From the day that Bill brought that stranger to my home, a series of events occurred that enlightened me as to the depth of trouble in which Bill found himself. Examples included the length of time that Bill spent in the bathroom, and upon his exit from said bathroom, the smell of a chemical that lingered in the bathroom and then followed him down the hallway as he advanced to the living room, where he slept. I had smelled that before. Crack cocaine. I don't know how many nights Bill took my car in search of crack cocaine while I slept. All I know is that the following morning my car had less gas than I remembered leaving in it, but I still didn't think that Bill had a problem.

The plan that Bill had described regarding the length of time he planned to stay with me did not pan out as he had communicated to me. After the first week, he asked if he could stay another week and then after that week, he asked to stay an additional week, in which I agreed. For the most part, I enjoyed Bill's company. After Bill did not leave as planned, I introduced him to two of my friends, Stacey and Juanita. He had already met the neighbors who lived in the apartment beneath my apartment, Carol and Teresa, and my neighbor, Pony, who lived two apartments down from my apartment. Quite often, Stacey had cookouts at her house and invited Bill, Erika, and me.

One morning while we were at work, Stacey called. "Hey, girl, what are you doing?"

"Not much. Why? What's up?"

"Let's go smoke a cigarette."

"Okay, I'll meet you outside."

When I saw Stacey sitting at the table where we normally smoked, I plopped down across from her. "What's up, chick?"

"Girl, I thought that you might want to know that Bill stopped by my house this morning at about 4:00 hoping that I could loan him $5.00 for gas to put in your car."

"What? Girl, you're kidding me?"

"No, I'm not kidding. I figured that you didn't know, so I thought that I should let you know."

I was bewildered by her news. "Girl, I think that Bill may be on drugs. Remember that stray guy he brought to my house? I'm thinking that him being at my house had to do with drugs as well."

"Yeah, I think that he's involved in drugs too. And that guy probably hooked him up with a drug dealer, or he may be the dealer himself."

Stacey and I sat outside for another ten or fifteen minutes before going back to work, but my mind remained in a daze from the news that she had given me. Her news had confirmed that Bill had been sneaking out in my car as I slept.

Bill also wrote two fifty dollar checks on my checking account, which caused my account to be overdrawn. In other words, he stole my checkbook! This incident hurt me the most of anything that Bill did to me. No mere words could describe my devastation.

Now the truth surfaced! Bill could not return to work because he continued to use drugs, thereby not allowing himself sufficient time for his body to metabolize the drugs so that he could pass the drug test if subjected to one upon his return to work.

I did not know what to do to help Bill, but what I did know hurt me to the core. I had to accept the fact that Bill had a serious problem that I could not solve or even help him resolve and that he could no longer stay at my house. I did not have it in me to kick him out on the street. Our friendship meant too much to me, and I knew that the real Bill I'd always known needed something beyond what I could offer. This Bill could not give me the shirt off of his back, he could not protect me, nor could he be my friend and my brother because he could not be his own friend under these conditions.

One day while at work, thoughts of the conversation I knew Bill and I had to have preoccupied most of my day. The moment I walked into my house, I brought up Bill's situation and my dilemma. "Bill, remember when we were walking in the park and you mentioned that you had gotten shot, but you didn't want to talk about it?"

"Umm, yeah, why do you ask?"

"You didn't want to talk about it because you didn't want to tell me about your drug problem, am I correct?"

Bill's body shifted, and he hesitated before answering. "Well, man, that dude tripped on me."

"Don't lie to me! I'm not up for that shit! Tell me the damn truth, or you and I are gonna fall out like we have never fallen out before, and I'm not bullshitting you! Tell me the damn truth now!" I meant what I said.

"Okay, yeah, I sold him some dope, and I added more baking soda than I should have so that I could make a little more money on the side. The guy found out, and we had an altercation, which led to him shooting me."

"So, it appears that you're in this dope game deep. You're lying and stealing because of it. And you're stealing from me? You're in deeper than you think."

"I'm not stealing from you!"

41

I called him out on his bullshit. "You're lying! You stole my car, and you wrote two fifty dollar checks on my checking account. If that isn't stealing, what the hell do you call it? And don't say borrowing because you didn't even bother to ask me if you could use my car! And you didn't ask me for a loan! But you know what, that's neither here nor there because I'm not doing this. You know that I love you like a brother, and I would never kick you to the curb, but we must nevertheless figure out a way for you to leave here."

"I know. I did have this one thought. Naw, don't worry about it."

"What?"

"Well, maybe I can do a slip and fall."

"A slip and fall? How do you do that?"

With a feather-brained gaze, he elucidated. "You know, I could go into a store and accidentally slip and fall."

"On purpose?"

"Umm, yeah. All I need to do is to drip some dishwashing liquid on the floor, act like I slipped on it, and then sue the store. With the money that I make as a regional manager, a lawyer could get me enough to not only repay you and fly home, but to help me pay off some of my other debts."

"So, you'll get enough to pay back the $100.00 for the two checks you wrote, your living expenses while you were here, and buy yourself a $200.00 one-way ticket back to New Orleans?"

"Yeah, and I'll give you enough for you to put some money in your pocket. With my income, I'm thinking they'll settle out of court for about $90,000.00 to $100,00.00 especially if I go to physical therapy. It'll take about six weeks for me to complete the physical therapy and about two or three weeks after that to receive the money. What do you think?"

"Are you serious? I was gobsmacked.

"As a heart attack."

"Which store?"

Bill scratched his chin, in thinking mode. "I don't know yet, but it needs to be on a day when we do the normal grocery shopping. That way we'll have a lot of food to check out, and it won't look like we're there only to run a slip and fall scam."

"I don't know. That's serious scamming. I've never done anything like that before. What if you get caught?"

"I won't. Trust me."

We sat there in silence for the rest of the evening pretending to watch television, but I know that neither of our minds could quiet down, as if we had not just had a conversation about scamming a store.

I lay awake that night, sleeping only intermittently. The blaring of the alarm clock startled me. *Time for work already? It's hard to fathom that eight hours have passed, and I've barely gotten a wink of sleep.*

For the next few days Bill and I discussed the slip and fall idea, and I knew that it had taken up residence in both of our minds. I tried thinking of other ways to generate the money needed for Bill to leave, but I couldn't think of one other idea. With Bill's drug addiction, I doubt he had established good credit or even had a good credit score so he couldn't borrow the money. In fact, I don't recall him ever using a credit card. In addition, he did mention that he lost his checking account due to him writing too many insufficient funds checks. He had a high income, but no credit and my finances weren't that great due to me filing bankruptcy and trying to reestablish my credit rating.

After pondering on my options, I finally concluded in my mind that I would go along with Bill's plans. I even prayed to God and admitted that what Bill wanted to do was wrong, but I could not think of any other way, so I needed Him to forgive me. I knew, though, that I could not continue to live in paranoia, constantly watching my belongings, worrying about my home while I was at work, and staying up all night keeping an eye on my car. I felt like a zombie most of the time. This had to end sooner rather than later.

Almost two months after Bill showed up, Bill and I pulled the biggest scam of my life, not that I had attempted any other scams. On the day of the scam, which was a Saturday, my normal grocery shopping day, Bill and I drove to my local grocery store and shopped as I usually shopped.

On a typical shopping trip, I usually spent two to three hundred dollars on all of the items that both Erika and I loved to eat, and I even splurged from time to time. But on the day of the scam, I couldn't splurge. However, I did get enough to last for the rest of the month.

While checking out, Bill blurted to the cashier, "Excuse me, ma'am. I'm buying pancakes, but I forgot the syrup, so I need to run and get it. What aisle is it on?"

"It's on aisle 17, sir."

"Okay, thanks." Bill sprinted to aisle 17 while the cashier and I continued talking and checking out. Less than five minutes later, a man announced over the intercom that there was a slip and fall on aisle 17. After another minute or two Bill had not returned, so I suggested to the cashier that we move forward so that I did not hold her line up any longer. I moved my basket of groceries to the front of the store and waited for Bill.

Ten minutes later the store manager approached me. "Hello, are you Vivian Thomas?"

"Yes, sir."

"Bill wanted me to inform you that he has been in an accident and is completing paperwork to report his injury. He should be with you in another ten or fifteen minutes."

"Okay, but what happened? And where is he?" I feigned concern like a pro.

"He's in our office. He fell and hurt himself."

"Can you take me to him?"

"Sure. Follow me."

The store manager and I entered his office, where Bill sat holding his back, answering questions being read to him by one of the store's supervisors.

I stepped into the office. "Bill, are you okay?"

"I don't know. I slipped and fell. I think that I slipped on some sugar. One of the stockers saw it and helped me up, and now my back is hurting. At first, I didn't feel anything, but after sitting here, I can feel it stiffening. I'm almost done, so I'll be out shortly."

"Do you need help getting to the car?"

"I don't think so."

"We'll get him to the car if he needs help, or we can call an ambulance if he feels like he needs to go to the hospital." The store manager made a kind offer.

"Okay, thanks, sir."

Ten minutes later, Bill appeared, leaning heavily on the store supervisor's arm as he inched himself to the car, his face a study in excruciating pain.

Bill and I rode most of the way back to my apartment in a discomforting yet satisfied silence. Neither one of us liked what we had just done, but we both felt it necessary for us to move forward. Though Bill did not articulate it in words, I could feel in his silence the hurt and disappointment that seared his soul.

"Bill, you said that you slipped on some sugar, right?"

"Yeah."

"I thought that you planned to slip on dishwashing liquid."

"I did, but when going down the aisle to get the pancakes, I noticed the sugar and remembered that sugar always seeps out of the bag onto the shelf. I checked to be sure and as expected, I saw sugar lying on the shelf, so I decided sugar would be better to slip on. In order to slip on the sugar, I had to slide one of the bags of sugar toward the front of the shelf, pushing the sugar on the floor. I then spread the sugar around with my feet so that it would be easier to slip on," Bill explained.

I took in all that Bill had described and could see how sugar would definitely work better.

And as an afterthought, Bill mumbled, "I guess I thought with the pancakes, the sugar, and the syrup all being on the same aisle, the slip and fall would be more of a convincing coincidence."

"Man, I never would have thought of that," I admitted with a bit of amazement.

"Well, it's not my proudest moment."

"I know."

"Coincidently, the stock person turned onto the aisle just as I slipped and fell, witnessing me falling. That couldn't have been planned better. I didn't even have to ask him to be a witness. He's the one who helped me up and called the supervisor. Though I'm not proud of what I did, I do have to admit, it couldn't have gone smoother," Bill confessed with confidence.

Bill and I never again discussed what happened on that day. Two or three days later, Bill informed me that he had obtained a lawyer and had been instructed by his lawyer to undergo physical therapy for his back. A deep sense of disappointment overtook me after learning that Bill would be living with me for another six months or so and not weeks as we had imagined when contemplating the slip and fall scam. But in order to get a sizable amount of money, six weeks of physical therapy would not be long enough. *Could I make it six months dealing with Bill's addiction? And what about his job? Would he still have a job after six months?*

As it turned out, I endured and Bill attending physical therapy helped because it kept him focused, disciplined, and away from any noticeable devious behavior. I do recall smelling crack cocaine a time or two, but I didn't find any evidence of him stealing from me after the scam. Bill did speak to his manager about him slipping and falling and could not return to work. His manager placed him on an off the job injury leave so that his job would be preserved for a minimum of one year.

At the end of the six months of physical therapy, Bill met with his lawyer, and he informed him that he had received a settlement offer. About a week later, Bill presented to me a settlement check in the amount of $80,000.00 for his slip and fall injury which was $10,000.00 to $20,000.00 shy of what he originally thought the settlement would be. Bill didn't complain because leaving California, particularly my home, was his primary focus.

I had never seen anything like that before. "Bill, is this check real?"

"Hell, yeah, it's real!"

"You got to be kidding! How did you get this much in just six months and a couple of weeks?"

"I could have gotten more, but I would have had to extend my physical therapy for a much longer period of time. I was paid for lost wages because, technically, I was still employed and couldn't return to work due to the injury as well as pain and suffering. Because my wages are high, I lost quite a bit each month that I could not work."

"Wow! I can hardly wrap my head around that!"

Before Bill left in December of 1992, he repaid all of the money that he owed me, and he even gave me $10,000.00.

"Angel, this money is to repay what I owe you, for Christmas presents for both you and Erika, and the rest is my way of apologizing for the trouble that I've caused you. I guess that it's compensation for your pain and suffering. And most of all, for being the angel that you've always been to me. I love you, Angel." He kissed me on the forehead and hugged me as if he knew that he would never see me again.

"Bill, I love you too. And thank you for taking care of me. What I want more than I can put into words is for you to promise me that you'll get help with your drug problem."

"Angel, I promise."

My relief was palpable. "Okay, I'm going to hold you to that. So, are you going back to New Orleans, or have you decided on somewhere else?"

"I talked to my dad. He moved to Nashville, Tennessee, so I'm going to go live with him for a while. I think that that'll be the best place for me to pursue recovery, and Nashville falls within my work region. But first, I'm going to go to New Orleans to grab my personal belongings, so I've purchased a one-way ticket to New Orleans, and then I'm going to rent a U-Haul with a hitch to drive to Nashville."

"Okay, well, you keep in touch and reach out whenever you feel a need to. You know that I'm all in. Whatever I can do to help, don't hesitate to let me know."

After Bill left, he called and let me know that he made it home, but after that, I didn't hear from Bill again until 1997, after I moved to Texas, which he informed me that once he settled in Nashville, a month after leaving California, he returned to his job as a regional manager in Nashville. I did hear rumors about him having issues with addiction, but you can't always trust what you hear. I hoped that he had kept his promise by getting the help that he needed.

Six months after Hurricane Katrina, the storm that devastated New Orleans in August of 2005, Bill called me. "Hey, Angel!"

A big smile spread across my face. "Hey, Bill! How are you?"

"I'm good, and the family is good. I'm still in Nashville, but my family is in Detroit until they can finish rebuilding their houses."

"That's good to hear. And how are you? How are you doing with your recovery?"

"Well, for a while I did good. After I left Nashville in 1998 and returned to New Orleans, it's like I couldn't get it together. I didn't want to get fired so, I quit my job, with successful performance reviews to ensure my chances of being rehired would be favorable if I ever decided to return to the job. I ended up spending a year and a half behind bars on possession with an intent to distribute charge. After being released, I couldn't stay clean, so I returned to Nashville and began a drug program at my dad's church. It's still hard, Angel, but I'm doing it, one day at a time."

Hearing about Bill's progress warmed my heart. Even though the path hadn't been easy, he kept holding on. Bill talked about all that God had been doing in his life and told me that he had joined the men's ministry, hoping that he would continue to grow and get beyond his drug addiction. From 2006 to 2015 Bill would call and check in on me, quietly showing that he was determined to keep moving forward. He might be in a battle, but he would win the war.

So, when Betty, Bill's ex-wife, called me on March 4, 2015, it tormented my soul to hear that my brother had passed away.

"Hey, Viv."

I didn't recognize the person on the other end of the line. "Hi, who is this?"

"This is Betty."

"Hi, Betty! How are you?" I knew something had to be wrong.

"Not too good."

"Why, what's wrong?"

"Bill passed away."

"What? Passed away? How? What happened?"

Betty's voice dripped with anguish. "Honestly, Bill's heart failed. I think that it was the drugs. He kept trying to quit, but he couldn't. He was clean for months at a time, but then he fell off of the wagon and chased that dope again for a month or two, ended up in jail or sick. Then he stopped for a minute, but he went right back at it a month later."

"I knew that he had a hard time with drug addiction, but I hoped that he had found the strength to overcome it. Thanks for calling me and letting me know."

I couldn't talk any longer. My heart plummeted to the very depths of my soul, and my throat choked with sorrow. My dear brother and friend was no longer with us. But I knew that whatever pain had disabled him no longer reigned in his life. My brother and friend was free at last.

* * *

When I lived in San Jose from 1988 to 1993, Chico and I talked almost every day. He visited me at least once a year, and every visit brought joy to my spirit. After December of 1992, my communication with Chico ceased. Whenever I called, his voicemail picked up. I left a message each time, but I never received a response from him. After two months his mailbox was full, and I could no longer leave a message.

I became concerned about him and couldn't imagine what had happened that would prevent him from calling me back. Besides, I wanted to enlighten him as to my upcoming one-week visit to attend the New Orleans Mardi Gras festivities so that he could ensure his availability during my time in New Orleans. I decided to call his mom, who was a beautiful, petite lady with a heavy, broken Dominican Spanish accent.

Sounding bashful, "Hi, Mrs. Flores, how are you doing? This is Viv."

"Hi, Biv. I do well, dough, I feel exhaustion."

"I'm sorry to hear that. Mrs. Flores, I've been calling Chico and leaving messages on his voicemail for the last two months, but he hasn't responded."

Mrs. Flores sighed. "Well, is no good for Chico. He is bery sick, my lady. That is why I have exhaustion. I sit with him all night."

My heart fell to my stomach. "What is wrong with him?"

"Chico need liber donator bery much. He no makes it without it."

"Oh, my! What hospital is he in?"

"He is at the Methodist Hospital, on the sebenth floor, room 704. You go see him, correcto?"

"Yes, I will be in town for a week for the Mardi Gras festivities and will visit him then."

"Perfecto! I see him later and will let him know," she whispered as she fought back tears.

"Yes, let him know that I will see him soon and to take care of himself."

"I will. We talk later. Bye for now."

It didn't seem real, what I had just heard. All kinds of thoughts raced through my mind. I knew that Chico drank alcohol, but so did I and most of our friends. I never thought that drinking would affect him or any of our friends to the point where it would damage our liver. This was nine years after I had met Chico, which meant that his birthday awaited around the corner. He was about to turn 31. Liver disease for some-one under 50 sounded inconceivable to me, but I guess that my naiveté showcased how much knowledge I possessed in this arena.

Other thoughts assailed me about him dying and not being able to see or talk to him. I couldn't imagine a world without him in it. It didn't seem fair that the life of one of my closest friends could end so early. The news about Chico made me think about my own mortality and how short life is. I could be here one day and gone the next, one breath away from not being amongst the living.

As I later stood at Chico's hospital bedside, I wondered what had happened to him. He didn't even look like himself. His face had aged more than the nine years that had passed since we met, and no more than two years had passed since his last visit to San Jose in 1991. So, why did his face and his body seem so feeble, I couldn't fathom. He lay there, so still, weathered by life.

I needed to see his white teeth, but they hid beneath the pain and anguish visible on his face. I couldn't bear to see him this way.

I squeezed his arm. He lay there motionless.

I bent closer to his ear. "Chico, I'm here. Can you hear me?"

His mouth moved without making a sound. *That movement must be my imagination.* I heard the door open and saw an attractive lady in her thirties enter the room. Her hair shaved like a soldier with new growth that resembled peach fuzz, she greeted me with open arms, and enthusiasm brightened her face.

"Hi, I'm Charlie." She shook my hand with both of her hands. "I know who you are. I've seen a million pictures of you and Chico. All he does is talk about you and the old days. Oh, yeah, and he considers you to be his best friend. He planned to take me to San Jose to meet you. He's convinced that you would like me."

I knew that Chico had a girlfriend, but he didn't talk much about her. I knew her name, but he had never mentioned bringing her to San Jose. His relationship with her seemed to me to be more casual than exclusive. If Charlie's words were anything to go by, a change must have occurred since Chico, and I had last spoken.

"Yeah, he's like a brother to me, and what's happening with him is so difficult to accept. It doesn't feel real. This illness leaves him like this, just out of the blue?" I pointed toward the bed.

Charlie dropped her head. "Chico's been sick."

"What do you mean, he's been sick?"

Charlie guided me by the arm closer to the door. "We need to talk. When you're done visiting, do you want to have lunch or drinks?"

"Yeah, that would be nice, cause I'm starving. I rushed over here without eating, so, yes, by all means, let's have lunch."

Charlie and I visited Chico for an hour. He never woke up, despite both of us trying to wake him. Two or three nurses checked on him, administered more medicine, and wrote notes regarding his condition to pass on to his doctor.

One of the nurses saw us trying to wake him. "Oh, honey, he won't wake up. He's sedated, and I doubt if he will wake up any time soon. He underwent a series of tests not long before you all showed up, which is why he's still unconscious. I don't expect him to wake up until tomorrow morning."

"Well, Charlie, since he won't wake up any time soon, let's pray and then leave for lunch."

"Sounds good to me. Oh, ma'am, thanks for the information. It's appreciated," Charlie whispered to the nurse.

The nurse continued attending to her notes. "No problem, hon."

Hon is an endearment used by many New Orleanians.

We prayed for Chico and left.

Instead of eating at a restaurant, Charlie and I decided to take our food out and have lunch at my mom's house. When we entered the house, we found that the residents of the house had already left, which gave Charlie and me an opportunity to share some uninterrupted time together.

As we sat in the yard eating, Charlie's admiration for my mother's backyard could not go unnoticed. I, too, had always loved my mother's backyard, even during my junior high and senior high school years. I always felt such peace and tranquility there. Many nights I sat in that backyard, talking to God, pretending that I lived in the Garden of Eden described in the Bible.

One night as I sat in the backyard, I must have been 15 or 16 years old, I prayed to God to shine a light in one dark area of the backyard, one in which Satan tried to make me fearful. And, from that night until now it seems that there's a constant shine of the moon in that area that eliminates the darkness.

Even then, though I didn't know what following Christ and being devoted to God meant, God answered my prayer. Whenever I question

God's faithfulness or I am navigating some storm in my life, I think of this incident as evidence of how faithful God is.

"So, Charlie, how did you and Chico meet?"

Charlie covered her mouth and swallowed the food in her mouth. "The company I worked for, when I lived in Florida, sold supplies to Mr. Flores' company.

"After I opened the store here in July of 1990, Chico picked up his dad's order every month, sometimes twice a month. When he first picked up the supplies, he acted kind of uppity or stuck up. After three or four times of picking up the supplies, I sensed that he didn't want to be there, though I didn't know the nature of his problem. After three or four months, I guess he figured out that acting uppity or rude would not change the situation, so I think that he decided that the being-nice option would serve him better, or perhaps the approaching Christmas season softened his heart. At any rate, to my surprise, he spoke to me. Two weeks after that, he joked with me. I never expected him to be so funny and witty. I loved that version of him."

I chimed in. "Now, that's the Chico I know. He always has a joke. From day one, he joked and acted silly with me. The first day we met, we talked for hours, and most of that time he incorporated jokes and funny stories about himself and his family into our conversation. That boy kept humor at the forefront of his personality."

Charlie's eyes agreed as she continued telling her story, "Well, after two months of being Mr. Nice Guy, he invited me to one of his friends' parties. I had so much fun that night. From that night forward he invited me to other places, like the movies and family gatherings. He even attended events that my family or I held. Before I knew it, we slept together, intimately that is. Then I fell in love with him.

"After a year of having an intimate relationship with him, I noticed his moodiness. At first, I thought that familiarity had kicked in, or perhaps he had met someone else he found more interesting than me.

"But, whenever I brought up whether he wanted to be with another person, he deflected and suggested that perhaps I wanted to be with another person. I couldn't figure it out. Some days I experienced the funny, loving Chico, and other days he acted indifferent or preoccupied, as if he didn't want to be bothered. At one point, I thought that maybe he could be depressed, but I didn't know for sure." Charlie stopped to take a sip of her wine.

"Then, sometimes he disappeared, and I did not hear from him for a week, sometimes two weeks. I called him, and he did not respond. I felt disrespected, especially when he promised that he would call me and didn't. After the second time that he failed to call me, as he had assured me he would, I asked him about it and let him know my true feelings about how his actions affected me. I told him that under no circumstances did I deserve to be treated that way and that I would not tolerate him or anyone else treating me that way. I loved him, but not enough to be disrespected!

"Then one night, at this party that he invited me to, he left me sitting alone while he ventured off to a room that he referred to as the back room."

I interrupted Charlie. "Oh, yeah, I remember the back room. This was the room where folks who wanted to snort cocaine and smoke crack hung out. Many of them stayed there for the entire party."

Charlie nodded in agreement. "So, you know what I'm talking about. At first, I didn't realize what the room was, but after half an hour had passed, I wondered what he could be doing that took so long. I searched for Chico and found the back room and learned, that night, that he smoked crack."

"What? You saw him smoking crack? He had the pipe up to his mouth pulling off of it?" I blurted out, aghast.

"Yep! I saw him hitting the pipe with my own eyes. After I saw that, I knew what the hell had been going on when I didn't hear from his ass for days at a time. I had a friend in Florida on that shit, so I knew enough about it to know that that was not a road that I wanted to go down.

"Initially, I decided not to deal with his ass anymore, but you know how it is. I loved him and figured that he had it under control because

54

he did take care of his business and all. I thought that he used it to take the edge off.

"Not! Girl, a year later, that shit took him places he didn't want to go. He lost control, and before I knew it, he stopped taking care of himself, he was out hustling for money, and he lied about his whereabouts and how long he would be gone. He became a person that neither I nor his family could rely on. I wanted to walk away more times than I could count, but I just couldn't. I knew his heart, his goodness, and I enjoyed his company...most of the time."

Charlie's eyes reflected her sadness. "I wanted the Chico I fell in love with; and I thought that if I stuck by him, I could help him triumph over his addiction. I hoped that he would realize the impact that the crack had on him. But that shit kept him hooked until he found out that he had liver issues. When he found that out, he sought professional help to overcome his addiction. He did well most of the time, except on the days when he suffered with the symptoms of his liver problem."

"What kind of liver problem does he have?"

"He has cirrhosis of the liver."

"Oh, my." I gasped.

I thought out loud as I searched my mind for clarity. "You know, I think that he has always suffered with liver problems. I can almost recall him mentioning having to go to the doctor as a child regarding his liver, so it might not be all drugs. The drugs may have aggravated it, though."

"I'm sure that the drugs didn't help." Charlie scratched her chin.

"Particularly since drugs tend to be toxic to the liver. The liver plays a major role in metabolizing and filtering substances like cocaine and crack once they enter the bloodstream," I added.

"Umm, I didn't know that" Charlie confessed.

"Damn! He never mentioned to me that he smoked crack. I knew that he snorted a few lines of cocaine or even laced some in a cigarette or a joint but not crack. So, I bet that that's the culprit behind him not being available every time I called. Whenever I questioned him, he just said that he was on the run and busy. I assumed that he meant being busy with work. But it sounds like he meant busy chasing that shit."

"Yeah, you're right about that. Not to mention, busy working on my last nerve. But, you know, I burned my brain out trying to figure out what was going on with him. I even talked to his mom about it, but she claimed that she didn't know his business like that," Charlie rolled her eyes to the back of her head.

"But most people who do that shit to themselves have deeper issues inside. He never went into detail, but he's broken down a few times and made statements like he couldn't deal with this shit or that shit anymore. He never gave me specifics, so I'm not sure what he meant, and whenever I probed deeper about his feelings, he shut down."

I recalled the same thing. "Yes, he used to vent to me too, but he kind of rambled on, so I didn't know the details behind his ranting. After a while, I stopped trying to figure it out and decided that what he needed most from me was to be a listening ear. During his breakdown episodes, he never acted like he wanted my advice, so I never gave it to him. My listening proved to be the antidote for whatever feelings were weighing on him because afterwards he joked about it, and then normalcy resumed." I felt the tears gathering in my eyes.

Chico's burdens and his condition seemed to have had a sudden impact on my emotions. My inability to swallow, because of the tears, choked me.

"Yep, that's the same way that he acted with me." Charlie's face scrunched in pain.

As Charlie watched me attempting to evade my emotions, her body language betrayed her own attempts to keep her emotions in check.

Charlie and I ended our conversation, and I walked her to her car. Glad that we had talked, I then better understood Chico's situation, which I felt would make seeing him again more manageable for me.

Later that night, questions such as, *What happened that made Chico want to smoke crack?*, and *Why didn't I already know?*, refused to leave me in peace. Chico and I had a close relationship. Shouldn't I have *sensed* his drug addiction? I thought about all of the times that he had pushed me off with excuses as to why he couldn't talk and the times that he claimed that he would call me back but didn't. The stampeding thoughts made my head throb with unbearable pressure.

As I lay in bed pondering these questions and more, the what ifs and should haves, and thinking about Chico and the old days, the thought of him dying crept in and took control of me and ushered me into a night of sobbing before drifting off to sleep.

I made it to the hospital by 10:00 a.m. the following morning, still tired from the night before. Chico flipped through the channels on the television mounted high up in the center of the wall facing his bed.

"Well, hello, handsome man, lying there pretending to be sick so that all of these pretty nurses can pamper you. You're not fooling me." I teased Chico with a light sense of humor.

Chico dropped the remote control as his head suddenly twisted toward me. His face lit up with instant delight and surprise when he saw me. This took me back to the day that I first met him.

He spoke in that thick Dominican Spanish accent. "My girl, I knew it! I could sense yo' presence deep inside me. It musta' been my spirit or a sixth sense that whisper'd to me dat' you would be bustin' through dat doe any minute. I am seri'is! Now dat is some seri'is shit! Girl, ya betta' give me a hug!"

I hugged him, and before I could stop him, he forced me onto the bed and squeezed me so tight that I could barely breathe.

With the rest of the breath that I had left in my lungs, I squeaked, "Chico, I can't breathe!"

"Oh, baby, I'm sorry. I'm oberwhelmed to see ya'. It's been so long since I've seen ya, and I can't describe how much I've missed ya. I've been so antsy from the time that I heard yo ass decided to visit a brutha'."

I sat on his bed. "Yeah, I talked to your mom a few days before leaving San Jose. After leaving a slew of messages on your answering machine and not receiving a return call from you, I was worried. It's not like you to not call, particularly when I have left a message. You always call me back."

Chico leaned into his pillow. "I know. Dis' sickness has been kicking my ass. I've been going through it. I've felt awful. At times, I felt like I was dying. Dis' pain has been unbearable."

"Why didn't you let me know?

He closed his eyes. "I guess that I just didn't wanna hear da words because I didn't wanna embrace the truf. And hear'in the words out loud confirmed dat I had a pro'blem dat I may not recoo'bah'ray from. I couldn't admit dat to you, not eben to me. Does dat make sense?"

I suppressed my grief. "You're gonna overcome this. God is not ready for you yet, He has too much work for you to do. You haven't even scratched the surface."

"Maybe so, but I didn't help Him. Dis is my doing. I poisoned my body for years. I didn't consider dis then, but I know now. I spent day after day and night after night regretting da stress I've subjected my body to." Chico sat up.

Chico picked up the remote and searched for the sports channel in silence. I think that we both needed the silence. We needed to lament for a moment while we each tackled our own inner thoughts. I pondered ways to bring up his drug addiction in such a way that wouldn't reveal that Charlie, and I had already spoken about it. At the same time, I fought the urge to fall into his arms distraught with sympathy, sadness, and uncontrollable sobbing. But I had to stay strong. If not for me, then for him.

Chico touched my hand. "I need to talk to ya', but I don't wanna talk in hea'. Do you think dat we could go to the bisitor's garden downstairs befo' da nurse brings my lunch?"

"Sure, we can. Do you need a wheelchair? Or will the nurse leave you to move around on your own without one?"

"I'm not bedridden, and my doctor prefer dat I exercise whenever I am able. But today, I'd rather bring da wheelchair 'cause sometimes walking wears me out. Besides, I'm used to ya pushing me around, anyway." He chuckled and scooted to the edge of the bed so that he could climb into the wheelchair.

"Boy, you are hilarious, do you know that?

"Yep, more than hell, cause hell can't compete with me!

I pushed Chico out of his room, down the hallway, and to the elevator. Chico charmed each of the nurses we encountered. The nurses were flattered by his flirtatious yet witty personality, and they blushed as we rolled toward the elevator. Chico joked on the entire jaunt to the visitor's garden.

When I stepped into the garden, the scenery, the atmosphere, and the tranquility of its beauty mesmerized me. The flowers and plants were arranged to create a warm, cozy, breathtaking ambience. Chico pointed toward the most private section of the garden, which was located at the corner of the entrance farthest away from the garden.

A stone wall separated this section of the garden from the rest of the garden. Behind the wall sat a table that could accommodate six to eight people. Chico positioned his wheelchair as far away from the entrance to that area as he could, and I sat across from him.

He clasped his hands together. "I'm so glad to see ya. I have play'd dis confo'sation dat we're 'bout to have ober in my mind a million times, searchin' for da right words. You have been closer to me than my blood family, and I know dat I can talk to ya. Ya may not have realized dis, but I have lived quite an unhappy life. You have no idea how many times I have thought about ending it."

"Are you serious?"

"Yes, I am seri'is."

"Why are you so unhappy?"

"I'm not now, but I have been fa most of my life. I lib'd a secrit life. You have no idea what I've wid'ness, what I've gone through, and what I've had to carry wit' me. From the age of 10, I've wid'ness kill'ins, tor'chure, and vi'lent threats wit' kno'in I could'nt tell nobody. It had to be secrecy to avoid disclosure to others, even doz' I felt close to, like you. Da people I loved da most have hurt me da most.

"I have spent my entire life sub'pressin fea' and angur. To drown out the sounds of deat', I drank, I smoked weed, I snorted cocaine, and I smoked crack, but none of dat worked. Instead of freeing me, I became enslaved to the kill'ers of my soul.

"And on top of dat, I have ruined my liber. Da bullshit I've had to go through, I wouldn't wish dat shit on my worst enemy. And now my ruined liber is taking its toll on me. According to da doctor, I need a liber transplant. One dat my body do not reject. But if it does reject it, dat won't bother me as much as having to lib with da faces and da voices dat I've witnessed tor'chured or kilt. Da life I've had to lib is not who I am, which is why lib'ing with dat kind of stuff ruined my chances for true happiness."

"But you always seemed so happy, always joking around, so enthusiastic, and full of life." I objected to his characterization of his life.

"Dat is how I cober'd my hurt, my pain, my fea', and my angur. I couldn't let people know how misa'ble I felt, my true feelin's. Too many people woulda been hurt and some eben ruined."

"Did you seek psychiatric treatment?"

"In my family, dat's ne'ber an option."

"Why not?"

"Too dangerous. Taking chances like dat couldn't be considered when you fac'ta in all da horrible stuff I had already wid'ness. Just like it happen to doz folks, it coulda happen to me or anyone in my family. Dat could have ruined my entire family."

"What about the priest? Did you try going to confession?"

"I felt like God had abandoned me and didn't care, so I blamed Him for my mis'ry and Him let'in me go through all of dat. In my mind, I couldn't figure out why God would do dat to a 10-year-old child who didn't ask to be born into such a horrible situation. I consider myself a noble kid, lo'bin and kind, and He did noth'in to stop me from wid'nessing others being hurt, even kilt. And not one time, but time after time. It pissed me off like you wouldn't eben know. I didn't want any part of God. I didn't trust or have faith in Him. How could I?"

I listened to him in utter silence because I didn't know that he felt that way about God. "But I've heard you talk about God over the years."

"Yeah, I did, to appease others."

My heart plummeted to the floor. He could not die as a non-believer. I caressed his hand. "You cannot die a non-believer. We won't see one another in the afterlife if you do, and I want to see you in eternity."

"And I won't die a non-believer. Ya see, God show'd me dat He had not abandoned me, dat He's been wid' me through all dat I've gone through. He helped me see dat He doesn't hold me accountable for others' sins, so I shouldn't hold Him accountable for da sins that I've wid'nessed and encountered because of the actions of others. Da sins that he holds me accountable for are my own sins. And blaming Him is da same as holding Him accountable for what others have done to me. God presented me with two questions. The first, should I be punished for what others have done? If the answer to this question was no, then why should I punish Him? And at dat moment, I fell to my knees cryin' and beggin' for His forgiveness. When I rose from the flo an hour later, all my angur and pain had vanished. For da first time in my life, I felt free. You know, I didn't feel any guilt, sadness, or shame. I felt dat my past had been erased."

Chico and I talked until the nurse interrupted us so that he could return to his room for his treatment. I had a million questions about what Chico had embarked upon me. When and where did he witness a murder? Who killed who? Did it involve a gang or the mob? Or did it involve his dad or one of his dad's business associates? But, for some reason, I didn't feel comfortable seeking additional information. I concluded that I should let him talk and be content with the amount of information he felt comfortable confiding in me with and it was all that I needed to know.

Though this was not typical of how I usually operated, probing further didn't sit right with me. In hindsight, my gut feeling is that my spirit intervened and wouldn't let me probe any further.

On our way to his room, we talked about his relationship with Charlie. He spoke about how he had always seen her as an honorable and loving woman. But his lifestyle had prevented him from giving her his whole heart. However, because of her faithfulness to him and the way that she had helped him cope with his illness, he wanted to give what was left of his life to a committed relationship with her.

"Charlie has done so much to help me. I'm considering marrying her. I hadn't planned to have children, but if it happens with Charlie that would be cool with me because it would be God's Will for sure." Chico grew enthusiastic.

"Yeah, we talked yesterday, and I really like her. She seems down to earth, and I think that you guys will do well together. As for children, that would be super because I think that that would give you a chance to be the dad you've always wanted. With all of the complaints that you've had about your dad, I'm sure that you will try your best not to make the same mistakes."

"You damn right about dat'!"

A month later the hospital discharged Chico, and he stayed with his mom as he continued to suffer with his liver disease. We talked at least two days a week throughout that time. We discussed his progress and his and Charlie's wedding plans every time we talked. Each time I could hear the joy in his voice as their wedding date approached. I could tell that he looked forward to his wedding day.

Chico and Charlie exchanged their marriage vows six months after Chico was released from the hospital in September of 1993. And shortly after this, Charlie was pregnant with twins.

In 1994 a suitable donor was identified, and Chico underwent a liver transplant operation. In 1995, Chico passed away because his body experienced a chronic rejection of the donated liver.

When I saw Charlie's number on the caller ID, I knew that Chico had moved on. I will forever miss him. Sometimes I hear that heavy Dominican Spanish accent in my mind so clearly that it feels like he's in the room with me. When that happens, my heart remembers my funniest and most loving friend, so it smiles with an ineffable warmth. Perhaps that's his way of letting me know that he's with me, even while he's resting.

* * *

In the spring of 1995, Lylah called. A rush of joy filled my heart when I heard her voice.

"Hey, Viv."

"Hey! What's going on with you? I'm so glad that you called!"

"Well, I'm better, but I do have some news that you might find upsetting. Are you sitting down?"

"Yeah, I'm sitting down."

Lylah took a deep breath. "Spence gave me HIV, which has led to my having AIDS."

She did not cry, nor did she appear to be angry. She delivered the news just as she always had, without mincing words. I had no response.

"I know that news like this is hard to hear."

I couldn't speak, so I remained silent.

"Hello, are you there? I need a response, a chuckle, a cry, a scream, I need some kind of reaction."

"Oh, Lylah, I'm...I'm so sorry." I sat there stunned; my chin hit the floor and my tongue felt dry as sand.

"Don't be. You didn't give me AIDS, Spence did. Don't be sorry for me. I am blessed because God gave me my own cause. I am fighting for my life and the lives of others. I am totally involved with making others aware of HIV and AIDS and how to live with HIV and AIDs. I'm working on awareness committees at various churches and community centers.

"I recently moved from New Orleans to Sacramento, California, with my parents. They decided to retire and wanted to do so in Sacramento. And since learning of my condition a year ago and coming to accept and cope with my reality, I decided that it would be easier for my parents and me if I moved closer to them, so I moved to Sacramento six months ago. You could not conceive the changes that I have had to go through. Girl, we have a lot of catching up to do."

"You have that right! First, the fact that you moved to Sacramento and didn't tell me prior to moving, well, that's just disappointing!" The hush in my heart that had threatened to overwhelm me diminished somewhat.

"Though I settled in Sacramento six months ago, my perspective and acceptance of my disease hindered me prior to moving. I found it easier to talk to strangers about my condition rather than talking to the people closest to me. I felt embarrassed, hurt, and depressed. It took almost a year for me to wrap my mind around it enough to work through my depression and find the strength and courage I needed to move forward. Getting involved with the many organizations that taught me awareness helped me the most. It gave me an avenue to address my deepest feelings with others who were experiencing the same circumstances."

Once she got started, Lylah couldn't stop. "You know, what I regret the most is smoking so much crack and trying to numb myself to the reality that the love that I had for Spence fell short of true love. I let that man do whatever he wanted to do in the name of love, and now, I know, that with Spence, I searched for love in all the wrong places. Neither he nor I knew the true meaning of love.

"Even within my own family, I didn't feel love. Hell, maybe I accepted the false narrative about love that television painted, and/or perhaps, I listened to too many love songs. It took AIDS to teach me a more realistic definition of true love. While working through my depression, I discovered God's love, and for the first time, I felt Him, and the feeling that I felt had to be love. He offered me an unspeakable peace, a sense of contentment that I had never felt before.

"If I had had this feeling years ago, I know that I wouldn't have needed any other high. But God doesn't make mistakes, so having AIDS must be my cause. Before my diagnosis of HIV and AIDS, I didn't have a cause. So, don't be sorry for me, be glad that I have found my cause, my purpose."

"My God, Lylah, now I feel sorry for me and ashamed that my initial thoughts didn't immediately acknowledge your strength and awesomeness. I should have known that you would rise to the occasion." My words flowed from my heart, dispensing the honor that I felt towards her.

"Well, I do have to admit, it didn't happen overnight."

Lylah and I talked for four hours that night. She informed me that her thinking and behavior had altered her character to the point that she didn't even recognize herself. She explained that she had moved in with Spence and that during that time he lost all respect for her.

"Girl, I hate to think about the way that Spence treated me and how I gave him permission to do all that he did to me simply because I wanted another hit off the pipe. You're my girl, so I can tell you. That fool had me sleeping in his shed like a dog. He used to throw a couple of rocks into the shed and call it snack time. And I, like a fool, fell to the floor, scrambling on my knees trying to pick them up. On a good day, we spent a little time together getting high, but whenever he got mad at me, he treated me like crap, from cussing me out to beating the hell out of me."

What she described made me feel a distinct disdain for Spencer. I couldn't even imagine that he would be so cruel to her. Her drug addiction caused her to stop going by her parents' house and their workshop, and it also prevented her from working. She preferred to avoid her parents so that she didn't have to hear their criticism about changes that she needed to make in her life. Another hit off the pipe stayed at the top of her priority list so that she could cope with her current situation. Spence took advantage of that because if she didn't work, her pay evaporated, which left her dependent upon him to get high and to meet any living expenses that she had.

Though Lylah had a serious addiction to crack cocaine, for a while she hid it from her friends and family. No one knew the extent to which Lylah's addiction had escalated. Choosing Spence to be her primary supplier and smoking solely with Spence and one or two other close friends enabled her to keep her addiction secret, thereby assisting her in keeping her reputation and that of her family intact which is why she used discretion in terms of from whom she purchased the drugs. She understood that though she chose not to show up for work at this time, she still considered designing to be her livelihood once she decided to resume working. She knew one day that she would; she just didn't know when. In addition, for Lylah, Spence meant limited chances to the likelihood of being arrested for possession of a controlled substance.

By the time that her relationship with Spence ended and she no longer lived with Spence, she did continue to buy crack cocaine from Spence. Knowing that she would not purchase from another dealer due to the necessity of keeping her addiction a secret and protecting her business reputation, Spence demanded that she have oral sex and sexual intercourse with him, which included anal intercourse, before he would sell the crack to her. He wouldn't accept her money, he deemed her money not good enough. But because her desperate craving for the drug overpowered her longing to be treated with dignity and respect, she accepted his terms.

Lylah's dealings with Spence ended when Lylah's brother, Breeze, found out the degree to which Lylah's addiction had escalated when Jake, Breeze's girlfriend's brother, blurted out, during an argument with Breeze, that Lylah and he used the same drug dealer.

Jake yelled at Breeze, "You need to mind your own damn business and focus on Lylah being fed crack treats by Spencer, lapping it up doggy style."

Breeze nearly lost his mind! His 3rd degree black belt in Karate meant that he hit Jake in places that Jake couldn't remember ever being hit in before. In a state of fury, Breeze beat Jake to within an inch of his life. He forced Jake to tell him where Spence lived.

Breeze sped into Spence's driveway, swerving to avoid running into the hedge located at the base of his driveway. Breeze jumped out of his car and dashed to Spence's door. Without knocking, Breeze blasted into Spence's house with a single kick to his front door. Breeze found Spence standing five feet away from him. Without hesitating, Breeze rushed Spence, utilizing five or six combination blows similar to the blows that the famous actor Bruce Lee used to throw at his opponents.

Panting, Breeze roared, "If I hear that you even talk to Lylah ever again, that will be your last time speaking because I'm gonna rip your tongue out, cut off your dick, and shove them both up your ass."

Breeze kicked Spence another two or three times. By the time he finished beating Spence, Spence had to be hospitalized.

After that beating, Spence knew that Breeze meant business, and Spence knew that Breeze knew the difference between a threat and a promise. Spence did talk to Lylah again, and he informed her that she needed to be tested because he may have given her HIV. He followed up with an apology for the way that he had treated her.

Spence introduced Lylah to crack cocaine, played a role in Lylah's addiction, and punished her for being addicted to crack cocaine. While Lylah accepted the atrocious way that he treated her, she did so all in the name of love. She never lost the importance of her career and her reputation. Though she tolerated his disrespect, she didn't consent to being destroyed.

I could hear in Lylah's voice when speaking about Sacramento that she enjoyed her time in Sacramento. She could live without reminders of her past as she maneuvered her way around. She met a nice guy who brought sunshine into her life. And she enjoyed working with the organizations that promoted HIV and AIDS awareness and prevention. She felt that her life, though she knew that she was at the end of it, now had the meaning for which she had always searched.

I visited Lylah during her time in Sacramento, and during my visits I could see that her life was a testament to joy, to the love of God and her family, and to the love of a man she admired and respected. Even on those days when she experienced excruciating pain, love shone through the darkness. Lylah's battle with AIDS ended in December of 1995. Though Lylah passed away, her work and her spirit live forever. And for that I am both thankful and amazed. Be at peace, my dear friend.

* * *

I have tried to illustrate here the characters and hearts of my three dear friends. I have intended for their stories to showcase the enormous hearts that they possessed; the genuine, endearing personalities of each of them; their sense of humor; and their generosity and kindness. I also hope that their stories delineate how each of their addictions altered their lives and took them to places outside of who they were and transformed their familiar characters into people I did not recognize.

All three of them came to operate outside of their normal behavior, which I'm convinced is always Satan's intent. Satan seeks to steal, kill, and destroy, which is what he did with my friends from the moment that their addictions took hold of them. The best qualities that they possessed prior to their addictions were the same qualities that God might have used for transforming hearts, minds, and souls. Unfortunately, my friends' addictions distracted them.

I remember hearing a sermon by Ron Carpenter, pastor of Redemption Church in San Jose, California, and founded in Greenville, South Carolina, where he preached that *Satan doesn't have to destroy you, he just has to distract you.* I found this to be a profound truth, as evidenced in the lives and deaths of my friends.

With this poem, I released from the deepest crevices of my soul what I felt after being informed of their deaths.

Crying Spirit

The tears wouldn't stop rolling down my face...
As my mind replayed over and over scenes of the past, of the memories.
Suppression did not work. Forgetting was impossible.
And praying only intensified my desire to cry.

It seemed as though my heart had stopped pumping blood.
And in its place, it pumped tears, tears of no color, no sound, no taste.
Tears of hurt, pain, despair, disappointment...
So, I swallowed, and the tears paused.

But only for a few moments, until they started to flow within.
They flowed across and over my heart.
They passed through my stomach.
And down my spine to my feet...

Quiet tears fill me, causing my organs to drown.
No relief, I felt no relief.
Until the dam of my eyelids burst with more tears.
And the tears wouldn't stop rolling down my face.

As my mind told me that the tears were good,
and they would bring healing to my soul.
You know, words from the Bible.
And healing...like salt to a wound.
And pulsating pain, indescribable pain.

Then the numbness set in.
Numbing the very breath that I breathed.
Breathe, I heard within, breathe...
So, I inhaled.

Air at last pouring into my tear-filled lungs,
Pushing the tears to my sinuses, and
Underneath my closed eyelashes so that when I open my eyes,
I discovered my tears rolling down my face...

They wouldn't stop.
But these tears appeared to have color,
so bright that it was tranquilizing and full of peace.
There was sound so soothing that it blew over me,
the breath of God calming and so comforting.
And astonishing taste, made my taste buds want to dance and rejoice...

Now, ever so subtle, I could feel the healing.
I felt the healing.
When my spirit cried,
I felt the healing.

So, I just lay there...
As my spirit cried and cried.
I just lay there...
Until the tears stop rolling down my face.

I miss you all and will always love each of you.

CHAPTER SIX

ASSIGNMENT PREP: KNOWING MY CREATOR

As far as I can recollect, God has always been a part of my life. As I mentioned in Chapter One, my mother trained her girls in the way that they should go, as instructed in the Word of God in Proverbs 22:6 (NKJV). We attended Sunday School, Bible study, Vacation Bible School, and Sunday church, which is how my mom ensured that the seed for spiritual growth would be planted in her girls. Once planted, God would do the rest by nurturing and growing us into the people He wanted us to be and by giving us the talents and gifts that He needed us to have to accomplish the tasks that he intended for us to accomplish.

In fact, sometime in 1974, when I was 11 years old, I visited a sanctified church in Los Angeles, California, when visiting my Aunt Bobby's friend. I cannot recall the name of the church, but I'll never forget jumping up and clapping my hands to the drums and tambourines being played while the congregation praised Almighty God.

The row in which I sat included me, my aunt and her friend, my sister, and two of my cousins. I don't recall my family nor my aunt's friend engaging in praise in the same manner as the other members of the congregation were, all of whom were dancing, jumping, and running around. Besides, me, the other children in my row, my sister and two cousins, gazed ahead or interacted with one another while the adults in my row sat and absorbed what appeared to be an experience of intense pleasure.

And then a sudden and unexpected force lifted me out of my seat and planted me on my feet, declaring that I could no longer be a spectator. Yes! I was forced to stand and give praise in the same manner in which the others in the congregation gave praise. I stomped my feet, clapped my hands, and sang praises unto the Lord.

My aunt and the others who sat in my row laughed in amazement that I, a mere child, participated in such a scene. I endured years of storytelling about the day that I jumped up, clapped my hands, and praised God while at that sanctified church. Unbeknownst to me, a change in me occurred. For years I could not explain what changed, but now I contend that the spirit that moved me to stand and praise God is the same spirit that God vowed to nurture and feed throughout my life.

I didn't know God's plan for my life when I visited Los Angeles, but by the end of our visit, I became certain that, in the future, I would reside in California. I lacked knowledge of when, where, or how, but I remained certain that I would.

Two years after my visit to Los Angeles, because of the foundational teachings of my mother and the many Sunday school teachers at church, I received the sacrament of baptism.

At the age of 14, I encountered a more structured and profound exploration of God's Word, which offered to me a more comprehensive and expanded awareness. The Spirit of God, in a moment of boredom, led me to read some books that my Aunt Bobby had given my sister, Shauna, as a gift, namely a twenty-six-volume set of Bible stories. To my knowledge, I am the only individual in our household who ever read all twenty-six volumes.

While passing by the bookcase, I noticed those books, and because of my apathy on that day, I decided to read one of them. Following the first book, I delved into the second, captivated by the intrigue of the initial volume. The curiosity intensified after the second book, compelling me to carry four books simultaneously upstairs to my room for my continued delight.

By the time that I completed reading all twenty-six books, I had read the Bible like an engrossing narrative, covering everything from the creation to the glorious return of Jesus, spanning his departure from this earth to the eventual establishment of the Kingdom of Heaven. Acquiring this knowledge enhanced the experience that I had had in Los Angeles and made me hunger for more.

Eleven years later, in January of 1988, I purchased a one-way ticket with money earned running errands for one of my uncles, and I moved to San Jose, California. Once in San Jose, I stayed with a friend from high school. The following day, a temporary agency assigned me to a temporary job at National Advanced Systems.

On the second day of my employment, I overslept because of jet lag. A representative of the temporary company I worked for called me to inquire about why I didn't show up for work. I told her the truth, explaining that I didn't have an alarm clock, that I had just moved, and that I had overslept.

She responded that the manager to whom I reported liked me and requested that I return.

I thought to myself, this is unreal! Thanks to God's favor, I could resume the job. Two months into my employment at National Advanced Systems, I moved into my own apartment. Four months later, I faced a layoff due to the plant's closure. However, my manager informed me that someone at the parent company, National Semiconductor, wanted me to work at corporate headquarters. God granted me everything essential to my life, carefully selecting for me a career in accounting, a reasonably priced apartment, and a place of worship.

In August of 1988, He granted my most crucial need, the anchor that I needed for Him to inaugurate His work, in the person of my daughter. Erika would be nearly 7 years old by the time that she joined me in California. Since I didn't initially have a place of my own or a job, I thought that it would be best if Erika stayed with my mother until I had found a safe and secure place for her to live. Three months passed before I felt like I could send for Erika, but the school year hadn't ended, so my mother agreed to keep her until the start of the new school year in San Jose. It worked out perfectly because my oldest sister, Deanne, and her friend flew to California with Erika, so I didn't have to fly to New Orleans to pick her up, and she didn't have to fly to San Jose alone.

It is my contention that Jesus serves as our heavenly anchor, while on Earth, God appoints us an earthly figure, to whom I refer as an earthly anchor, to help us maintain stability and remain centered and focused. This figure could be a child, a sibling, a relative, a friend, a neighbor, a pastor, a church, or even a stranger. Over my lifetime, my anchors have been and continue to be my mother, my father, my sisters, my daughter, three or four close friends, and my husband.

We all need anchors in our lives. God's Word declares that it is not good for us to be alone. Many relate this strictly to marriage. While not all folks are destined for marriage, the universal calling for each of us is to illustrate love toward one another. And, through loving one another, and being an anchor, we can portray love by fulfilling the essential role of offering the help that we all need.

The bible states,

> *And the Lord God said, "It is not good that man should be alone; I will make him a helper comparable to him."*
>
> Genesis 2:18 (NKJV)

The Amplified Bible describes it as suitable. What this signifies to me is that God ensures that we receive the necessary help from a willing and capable helper. And it is this helper who keeps us from facing life alone.

Erika, as my anchor, kept me focused and rooted; her as my responsibility, kept my toes on the ground. She prevented me from giving up because I knew that God had selected me to nurture her to live a life in which she could trust, rely, and depend on Him. He knew that this would not be an easy task for me since He had not completed my own development in living a life where my complete trust and dependency on Him had proven to be unshakable. My mother had ingrained within me the essential groundwork, and as an adult woman, her role had shifted from caregiver and nurturer to that of a pillar of encouragement.

He knew the seasons that I would face, the obstacles and hardships that I would endure, and the accomplishments toward which He would direct me. And He knew that the lessons that I needed to learn would be taught via college, Bible study, and living. He also understood the lessons that I needed to impart to others before and after the accomplishments that he had prepared for me could come to fruition.

So, from the quickening of my spirit, which was characterized by a heightened awakening of my emotions, thoughts, and a profound sense of vitality, to the symbolization of baptism, and from beckoning me away from my familiar places and comfort zone to ensuring the fulfillment of my fundamental requirements, God had acquainted Himself with me. And, He had positioned me for further development with the intention of using me in accordance with His purpose.

God called me out of familiar places because He knew that if He hadn't, I would have continued down a destructive path, making choices that would have ultimately blocked or delayed the fulfillment of His Divine Will for my life — even with the spiritual encounters I experienced from time to time.

One of those spiritual encounters happened in my early twenties. I had joined Nazareth Church of God and Christ and had requested to receive the Holy Spirit through one of the tarrying services, which is a service where one calls upon the Lord to fill her with His Holy Spirit. Maternal figures who are often referred to as mothers of the church stood alongside me to offer any assistance I may have needed.

After an unspecified duration, I felt a rushing wind enter the room, which knocked me over. I have a recollection of an organ cover being placed over the bottom half of me, as my dress lifted above my bottom, and one of the church mothers aimed to avert any visibility of my private parts. Upon rising from the floor, I experienced a sensation of being weightless, light as a feather. I returned home and phoned a friend, recounting my whole experience during the tarrying service. I didn't mention it to any of my family members out of fear that they might perceive me as being mentally unstable.

Fifteen years later, I read in the Bible,

> *When the day of Pentecost had fully come, they were all with one accord in one place. And suddenly there came a sound from heaven, as of a rushing mighty wind, and it filled the whole house where they were sitting.*
>
> Acts 2:1-2 (NKJV)

That night at the tarrying service, and even now, I don't recall hearing a sound, but I did feel a rushing mighty wind.

In 1985 while visiting two of my cousins at their home, we saw an angel standing on the moon with an emerald glow around it. The body resembled a man's body, but he had the wings of an eagle. Had my cousins not witnessed it as well, I might have presumed it to be a hallucination.

When studying God's Word, five or six years after moving to San Jose, I read another Bible verse.

> *And He who sat there was like a jasper and a sardius stone in appearance; and there was a rainbow around the throne, in appearance like an emerald.*
>
> Revelation 4:3 (NKJV)

After reading this I thought of the angel my cousins and I had seen.

Despite the spiritual encounters through which I perceived God's call for a closer connection, like the Bible story of Jonah, I continued along my personal path, which over time led me into the belly of my own whale. However, in contrast to Jonah, I lacked spiritual knowledge, which is why I feel that God chose to send me to San Jose. I think that He prepared to educate me and to show me His true nature, which is the reason why I refer to my period in San Jose as Boot Camp 101.

Relocating to San Jose fulfilled a cherished aspiration. Nevertheless, I have not detailed in the preceding chapters of this book the fundamental reason behind my decision to move. However, I am convinced that I moved in God's time and for God's purposes, but the motivation for moving at that moment, in January 1988, was my attempt to escape from an evil force by the name of Eli Porche, the individual I described earlier in Chapter Two. In hindsight, I now know that this man had had significant pain in his life, so much so that he permitted satanic forces to overtake him.

I met Eli in 1984 or 1985. He was an attractive guy, but his inner man laid bare the ugliness inherent to his personality. Eli was possessive and abusive. He had the audacity to be jealous of the fact that I had a father who lived in the same house as I did. After dating him for a year or so, I knew that I could not be with this type of person. My upbringing had not led me to encounter these kinds of circumstances, and I had no doubt that our relationship did not embody love. I knew that Eli's insecurities and jealousies would exacerbate the situation, so I understood that I needed to move on.

The tension around remaining in New Orleans stemmed from his threat to harm my daughter should I choose to distance myself from him. Thus, an idea struck me one day. I decided to feign interest in relocating to San Jose as a family of three. I opted for this strategy because I knew that I couldn't take my daughter with me, absent secure living arrangements for her. Leaving Erika with my mother seemed safer, as I didn't think that Eli would visit my mother's residence if he thought that I was planning for us to move as a family. I told Eli about a girlfriend residing in San Jose and explained to him my plan to travel there, secure employment, and find an apartment for us. I suggested that he and Erika could join me later.

Eli knew that I wouldn't permanently leave my daughter behind, and the period of separation from her would be brief, so he fell for it. After moving to San Jose and into my own apartment, he voiced his desire to join me, but he needed time to accumulate funds for the trip. I agreed. Because Erika remained in New Orleans with my mother, maintaining a polite demeanor with him became necessary in case he followed through with his threats.

I wished that I didn't have to give him my new address in San Jose, but he claimed that he wanted to send me mail, and I couldn't think of a way around giving him the address.

I had met the neighbors below me, and they were blessings of every kind. But Stacey and Juanita were my closest friends in San Jose, genuine friends on whom I could depend, and I am certain that they were additional anchors that God placed in my life to ride with me during both the calm seas and the raging waters that were sure to come. And if they ever needed me, I made it my duty and honor to be there for them. Our conversations always consisted of an extensive array of subjects.

My neighbors, Carol and Teresa, invited me to visit their church. At first, I didn't want to go because I didn't know the type of church that they attended. Upon walking into their church, following additional contemplation, what I witnessed astonished me. The church bore the name Prayer Garden Church of God in Christ, pastored by Pastor Paul Bates, an exceptional pastor. The church choir also delivered an impressive performance.

In February 1989, Eli called and informed me that he was on his way to San Jose to be with me and Erika. Two days later, he knocked on my door. Though I had hoped that I had escaped danger, and just when life seemed harmonious in my realm, I discovered that Eli, the devil from hell, had embarked upon a voyage of over twenty-two hundred miles just to torment me.

I often referred to Eli's coming as the beginning of God teaching me to address evil head-on, like a military soldier would combat an enemy set to destroy the life and property under his protection. I considered this period in my life to be comparable to Boot Camp because of the intensity, concentration, and focus required to learn God's ways, character, scriptures, concepts, and principals — all as they related to overcoming evil and stepping into my ability to possess supernatural powers through faith.

Upon Eli's entry through the front door, I sensed the presence of malevolence. I must confess that this frightened me at first, but in 2 Timothy 1:7, Timothy informs believers that God has not given them a spirit of fear, but rather one of power and of love and of a sound mind. Timothy's words served as a prompt for me, reminding me of God's previous actions on my behalf. He had placed me in an environment conducive to learning and empowerment, positioning me in a church guided by biblical principles and ensuring anchors of support to lean on when needed. God recognized my readiness to face this Boot Camp-like experience and spiritual trial. And now, it stood as my moment to acknowledge it too.

After a week of being in San Jose, Eli's evilness reared its ugly head by trying to rob me of my confidence. He attempted to isolate me from the friends I had made. He showed up at my job, in the van of the new company with which he had found employment, to make false accusations about the relationships that I had with my male co-workers. He hurled verbal threats at me. His ultimate strike came when he threw my glass punch bowl against the wall and then proceeded to chase me as I made my escape through the front door of my apartment.

Through prayer, equipping myself with the knowledge of God's Word, and meditation, God taught me to see beyond the person and instead to see that which inhabited the innermost recesses of that individual, and to rebuke it (Zechariah 3:2, Matthew 4:10 and 16:23, and Jude 1:9 (NKJV)) in the name of Jesus. Rebuking a demon involves compelling him to depart and yield to your commands. This is possible because God's Word says, *...He who is in you is greater than he who is in the world.* This scripture alludes to the concept that the spirit of God within you surpasses any forces present in the world.

So, I rebuked him using the name of Jesus. "I'm not afraid of you. What I'm afraid of is that one day I'm going to kill you and end up in jail for killing your nothing ass."

"What did you say?" Eli bellowed, as he propelled his body in my direction.

"You heard me, now shut up and lie down! Satan, I rebuke you in the name of Jesus!"

Astonished, I observed Eli settle down like a tired baby who had expended energy jumping around for hours. And right before my eyes, he fell asleep. I called that encounter a victory. I had rebuked the devil within him, and it resulted in him succumbing to my command. He had set out to steal my confidence through intimidation and fear, but instead, my confidence had increased, and my fear of him dissipated. In its place, I felt the fear of me killing him in self defense build.

Previous fights that we had had while in New Orleans always resulted in me hurting him. For example, one time he hit me at his cousin's house, and I hit him back with a heavy, solid body, made of cast iron or metal alloy type telephone, owned by his cousin. The manufacturing of these types of phones ended around the late 1970's to early 1980's. I gripped that phone in such a way that upon contact it put a gash in the middle of his head. Blood gushed out of his head like a waterfall. When he saw the blood, he knew that I meant business. He knew that if he didn't stop, I would kill him because he saw me reaching for a wine bottle. He could see in my eyes the dark death glare and the spell-like trance that I appeared to be under. He had no doubt that if he did not get out of that house in a hurry, he would be leaving in a body bag. Another time, in New Orleans, when he hit me, I hit him back by cupping one of my hands and hitting him on his ear. The cupping affect somehow caused his ear drum to burst.

Looking back on those other fights confirmed that the end of our relationship would likely be due to the death of one of us. And from the way that it looked, it would be his death, which is why I prayed that God would remove him from my home and my life. Through the time spent meditating and studying God's word, God had imparted to me the lesson that prayer made my requests and desires achievable.

God responded to my prayer by fostering a strong and compelling urge for me to move out of my bedroom where Eli slept to Erika's bedroom. On the first night In Erika's bedroom, I met his query about joining him in our bedroom with a refusal. The subsequent night brought the same question and an identical response.

On the third evening, he knocked on Erika's bedroom door. "You have no intention of joining me in our bedroom?"

"No, I don't."

To my surprise, he returned to our bedroom without causing a commotion.

The following day, after I returned from work, I found him with his suitcases packed, awaiting a taxi to take him to the bus station. A sense of sadness engulfed me after the realization hit me that I would be alone, even though I understood that his departure needed to happen for both of our sakes. However, it did take me by surprise that he folded so easily. I had expected him to raise hell, but he didn't, and my best guess is that my prayers and obedience to God forced him out because both God and I had agreed that it was time for him to go. The Bible states,

> ... *whatever you bind on earth will be bound in heaven, and what-ever you loose on earth will be loosed in heaven.*
> Matthew 16:19 (NKJV)

This verse is often interpreted as Jesus giving spiritual authority to man to declare what is permitted or forbidden. In Eli's case, his presence in my life had been determined to be forbidden so God ushered him out of my life for good.

In May of 1989, two days after Eli's departure, he phoned and requested that he be allowed to return. I declined this request. I understood that this stood as God's protection over me. God had taught me a lesson, that if I resisted the devil, he would flee from me James 4:7(KJV).

With the conclusion of that chapter in my life, God moved forward with disclosing His identity and expectations of me even further. He guided me toward the Old Testament of the Bible and introduced Himself as

the Lord God of your fathers, the God of Abraham, the God of Issac, and the God of Jacob and stated this is My name forever.
Exodus 3:15 (NKJV)

This introduction emphasized His covenant relationship with the patriarchs, and it established His name as eternal and worthy of remembrance.

He wanted me to know His name before revealing to me that His character diverged from what I had learned about over the years. He showed me His character, which embraced acceptance and love. He desired me to remain loyal to Him, and in exchange, He would become my God. Throughout my life I have always known that God had been my God, but what I learned was that He had been God but not my covenant God, until that point. And He showed up in a mighty way as I entered my BIG confrontation, an unrelenting financial dilemma.

When I left New Orleans, I had not given one thought to the real cost of living. I knew that I would have to pay rent and the energy bill, buy food, clothes, personal items, and furniture. I would even have to spend money on transportation. I hadn't really considered other essential items, such as cleaning products, linens, paper goods, and towels. This mistake contributed to my financial strain, along with the substantial telephone bills and the cost of dining out, which I did a lot of, even though I couldn't afford it. Being a single working parent, I grappled with the conflicting ideas of convenience and affordability that dining out presented.

Adding insult to injury, I befriended Mr. Credit Card and Mrs. Pay Day Loan, which proved to be my two worst enemies. At first, they wined and dined me. They had me thinking that I could manage my finances by making modest payments each month and all the while remain oblivious to how the high interest rates affected my overall financial situation.

My situation deteriorated to the point where I resorted to borrowing from Peter to pay Paul, but even that spiraled out of control. After a while, robbing Peter to pay Paul became futile because the amount that I owed Paul exceeded what I could borrow from Peter, John, Andrew, and Caleb, even if I resorted to robbing them all at the same time. I lived in childlike bliss for two years, which led me to being in over my head, stressed to my wits end, with creditors calling my home and my job and garnishing my wages.

I experienced a roller coaster ride from which I needed to disembark, leading me to seek solace in God. Sometime in June of 1991, I ultimately filed for Chapter 13 Bankruptcy. It took me more than two years to navigate these obstacles, but through divine guidance in grasping the concept of tithing, which is the practice of giving a specific portion of one's income, usually 10 percent, to a religious organization or charity as a form of financial support and religious obligation.

The Bible instructs,

> *Bring all the tithe into the storehouse, that there may be food in my house, and try Me now in this", says the Lord of hosts, "if I will not open for you the windows of heaven and pour out for you such blessing that there will not be room enough to receive it."*
>
> Malachi 3:10 (NIV)

This verse is often cited to encourage tithing through faith and trust that God will pour out blessings as indicated in scripture. This scripture resonated with my faith and conviction. It left me with a profound sense that I couldn't afford to skip tithing because of my desperate need of God's blessings. So, I became a devout tither, and as a result, my financial status improved. I did not become rich, but God ensured I had enough to meet my needs.

In addition, God guided me in assessing my financial situation by directing my attention to my spending habits, including the duration of long-distance phone calls, my dining expenses, and the use of credit cards instead of cash for items for which I could save money to purchase at a later time. Incorporating this behavior into my daily life enabled me to live within my means and taught me to control my credit card usage rather than letting a lack of control and impulsiveness dictate my actions. As I navigated this process and mastered self-control, at times, coping with the consequences of overindulgence became unbearable. During these times, and when feasible, I employed a coping mechanism that involved me simply going to sleep. On many evenings, I found myself in bed by 6:30 p.m.

As I continued to tithe, doors continued to open for me. In 1992, I enrolled into the college program offered by National Semiconductor after the Vice President of Finance, Bob Mahoney, convinced my manager to approve my request to enroll despite the fact that my educational pursuit did not include the field of Finance. His interference allowed me to enroll into the University of San Francisco' bachelor's program for Organizational Behavior which changed the course of my career forever.

By the end of 1993, my bankruptcy had concluded. I received annual pay increases at my full-time job, and I found a second job working during the summer months while Erika visited New Orleans. I worked four hours in the evening as a telemarketer for the Fairmont Hotel. With this part-time job, I managed to pay off creditors that could not be included in my bankruptcy, such as my landlord, family, and most friends to whom I owed money. Entering into 1994, I had become pretty much debt-free.

Even with my success in becoming debt-free, I still wrestled with the difficulty of reducing my telephone bill. This was hard for me because most of my friends and all of my family lived in places for which it cost money to stay in contact with them. It reached the point where I welcomed a $500.00 phone bill. Most of the time, the bill was $700.00 or $800.00. I had to make a change!

I prayed for more money, and God reiterated time and time again that He had already given me sufficient funds. The issue lay in how I managed it, particularly as it related to reducing my phone bill. UGH! I really longed for the company of my family and friends.

I am not certain when phone companies modified their long-distance policies to include flat-rate long-distance calling plans, which made the cost of long distance a part of the service or package purchased and not based on a per-minute basis, but this change gave me an option to select unlimited long-distance calling for an affordable fixed monthly fee. God had blessed me beyond measure! I could talk for a fraction of what I had previously paid. With the modification in the phone companies' policy, by the end of my seventh year in San Jose, I had crawled my way out of debt. And without even realizing it, I left checks from my part-time job uncashed.

Another door opened that would impact my future finances is that in 1994, I graduated and received my bachelor's degree from the University of San Franciso.

In 1995, my friend and spiritual advisor, Stacey, left California for Arlington, Texas. Before her departure, we both participated in a church gathering where an elderly woman made a prediction. She mentioned my future relocation to Texas and how my daughter would find it appealing. Interestingly, I had no prior acquaintance with this elderly lady. Although I had spotted her at one or two past church functions, we had never engaged in a conversation. Given this, except for divine insight, it remained a mystery how she could have any knowledge about my forthcoming sojourn to Texas, especially when I had not yet considered leaving San Jose.

In the early spring of 1996, I became a Sunday School teacher for teenagers 15 years old and older. Volunteering my time to help teenagers proved to be rewarding, and I feel that this contributed to the blessings I received — as a tithe of my time, alongside the financial tithes I gave.

Life proceeded smoothly with me helping the church teenagers gain a better perception of God and His desires for their lives. In June of 1996 God spoke to me by urging me and tugging on my heart to discuss with Pastor Bates the issue of the duration of church services. At first, I found it amusing. How could I ever convey this idea to Pastor Bates? But God continued to nudge me. Thus, I assured God that I would approach Pastor Bates if He granted me the opportunity.

One day after Sunday School, Pastor Bates motioned for me to join him outside the sanctuary. As I walked over to see what he wanted, I felt my heart pulsating in anticipation of our conversation. Two, nearly three years had passed since my initial visit to Prayer Garden and each Sunday the church service started thirty minutes to an hour after the structured time of 11:00 a.m. This late start caused church to end as late as 3:00 p.m. or even 4:00 p.m. This might not have been an ordeal if my Sundays hadn't started with a 9:00 a.m. Sunday School class, followed by sitting through 11:00 a.m. service for a couple hours, then going home to cook, getting ready for work, and making sure Erika was prepared for school the next day. My solution — skip 11:00 a.m. service and that I did.

So, there I was summoned to a conversation with Pastor Bates that he had no idea he would be having with me unless God, Himself, fore-warned him. After greeting Pastor Bates and exchanging the usual pleas-antries, he mentioned that he had noticed I'd been leaving church after Sunday School the past few Sundays, and he wanted to know why. I glanced skyward. *Is that opportunity knocking?*

"Well, Pastor Bates, church lasts for too long. You're not dismissing church until after 3:00 in the afternoon."

"I commence church when the people show up. I can't move forward without the people, right?"

"Pastor Bates, some people are here. I'm here, and your wife is here. Besides, if you begin on time, rest assured, the people will show up on time," I responded.

"You attend church one day a week, Sundays, and you're complain-ing about how long it lasts? It's not like you come on Thursdays to Bible study too," Pastor Bates argued.

"So, if I make it on Thursdays for Bible study, you'll start church on time?"

"Yes, I will," he retorted in a sarcastic tone.

So, the next Thursday, there I stood at church ten minutes early for Bible study. Pastor Bates stood and stated that some people thought that church lasted too long. So, church will begin at 11:00 a.m. this coming Sunday. He advised folks to please make sure that they were there on time.

That Sunday, most people missed the 11:00 a.m. service. As church dismissed, many people strolled up the steps of the church in complete astonishment, inquiring of members leaving as to the reason why every-one poured out of the church as if church had ended. When they found out that church really had ended, they left in utter amazement. But, the following Sunday, most folks attended the service on time. Pastor Bates remained true to his word. He conducted church as he had agreed that he would. And I attended both Sunday School and the 11:00 a.m. service.

I enjoyed attending Prayer Garden. God used Pastor Bates and his congregation to bless me in many ways.

In February of 1996, the temporary employees in my division received layoff notices and rumors of layoffs threatened me, as a full-time employee, within the division, as well, though they had not come to pass. With these rumors, I found myself praying at the altar every Sunday, petitioning God for the direction in which He wanted my life to go, as being laid off seemed inevitable. I had no certainty about my destination, but I felt that the time for me to depart San Jose lurked right around the corner. I didn't want to return to New Orleans. I thought that perhaps I could move to Atlanta. I had heard positive things about Atlanta. So, I prayed about it.

One Sunday, while at the altar, Pastor Bates whispered in my ear that God had responded to my prayer; but I didn't hear Him. The altar serves as the central point for religious offerings, prayers, and symbolic actions. It is often regarded as a sacred space within the church or place of worship. To hear that God had acknowledged my prayers, but that I remained unaware of His reply, left me astounded, utterly taken aback.

I mentioned my thoughts about this to my mother. "Mamma, Pastor Bates informed me that God responded to my prayer, but I didn't hear His response."

"Viv, tell me, upon concluding your prayers, do you rise right away, or do you remain in contemplation, awaiting God's voice?"

"I rise without contemplating or meditating."

"That's why you didn't hear Him."

"What? You've got to be kidding me!" I burst out, unable to hide my shock.

"No, think of it like you're conversing with me. If you posed a question and didn't wait to hear my answer, would you know my response?"

I acknowledged her question. "No."

"Likewise, you won't hear God's reply if you don't listen for it."

Later that night, following my prayer, I lingered in anticipation of God's voice, and I thought God conveyed His guidance to me which was to move to Austin, TX, but I still needed more clarity.

"God, am I hearing you correctly? I don't know even one person in Austin. I thought that perhaps Atlanta might be a great place to live."

I heard God speaking to me. *And who do you know in Atlanta? No one.*

"Oh, yeah, you're right." I couldn't help but find amusement in the validity of His observation.

The following day I phoned my mother and informed her that God had directed me to move to Austin, Texas. She reminded me that I had a cousin who lived near Austin. Subsequently, I reached out to my cousin, who kindly extended an invitation to stay at her house if I decided to explore Austin.

After eight years of living in San Jose — gaining deeper insights into God's character, His expectations for my life, confronting and over-coming Eli's intense spiritual demons, finding success in managing my finances, growing stronger in my faith, and dedicating my time to the church — and with layoffs looming, I found myself yearning for a transition into the next chapter of my life, whatever that might be.

In July of 1996, National Semiconductor implemented layoffs, and I landed among those affected. I received a substantial severance package, affording me the ability to relocate to any destination of my choosing. *Austin, Texas, or Atlanta, Georgia? To which should I go? God, I think you're saying Austin, but I'm still uncertain as to whether it's You or just my mind.*

One day I visited the National Semiconductor credit union to make a deposit. Upon exiting, God conveyed a second message to me. *Go to Austin. I have a home for you, a job for you, and a man for you there.* At that moment, the authority I felt coming from His words which penetrated my heart removed all skepticism; and I knew without a shadow of a doubt that Austin would be my next home.

After the fact, the elderly woman who had predicted that I would relocate to Texas popped into my mind. *Wow, her prediction came true!*

CHAPTER SEVEN

ASSIGNED POSITIONING

I was laid off from National Semiconductor on July 12, 1996, which led me to accept the invitation of my cousin Carolyn to stay at her house while I checked Austin out. She lived an hour north of Austin in Killeen, Texas. Before going to her house, I stayed with a different cousin, who lived in Fort Worth, Texas, for four or five days.

On the day that I landed at the Dallas-Forth Worth airport, the moment I stepped outside of the terminal, I could not breathe. It felt like I had stumbled into a furnace, an ever-burning incinerator. After three or four gulps of air, my breathing caught up to itself.

While in Fort Worth, I also visited Stacey, since she did not live far from where my cousin lived. I enjoyed being with Stacey, however, the scorching Texas climate proved to be lethal. Following visits with both my cousin and Stacey, Carolyn picked me up, and we drove to Killeen.

Three hours later, we pulled into the curved driveway of Carolyn's house. She escorted me to the room in which I would be staying. Carolyn, her husband, and her children treated me like royalty. Before retiring for the evening, Carolyn handed me the key to one of her family's spare vehicles, with which she said that I could explore Austin.

The next morning, I drove to northwest Austin, and I fell in love with it. It evoked memories of the place that I had dreamt about several times prior to my move to San Jose. In those dreams, I envisioned a place with generous expanses of lush, green stretches of land. Northwest Austin oozed purity and exuded a serene, hushed, and tranquil atmosphere.

I drove until I saw a sign that read, *Apartment Locators*. I turned into the driveway and entered the office, a space no bigger than a 10-foot x 12-foot box, but the lady behind the desk was warm and professional. We talked for fifteen minutes, and I completed the paperwork. She then chauffeured me around as we sought a suitable apartment.

After an hour of searching, we discovered the ideal apartment. The apartments resembled tiny cottages, which suited my preference, as I didn't want Erika to have to navigate an apartment complex on foot. Since people in this world sometimes exhibit peculiar and inappropriate behavior, I felt it would be safer for her to live in a more house-like structure.

The two-story four-plex that I selected had two bedrooms and two baths. We lived on the first floor, which gave us access to parking in the front and back of the cottage. The school that Erika would attend was roughly a mile up the street from where we lived.

After I selected my apartment, I submitted the deposit and then made my way to the school to enroll Erika for the upcoming year. This school, a welcoming public institution, upheld a high standard. Its neat, orderly appearance reflected strong financial support, which I felt had secured access to ample funds, assets, and resources. This backing offered the stability, security, and opportunities essential for both students and faculty members.

During a meeting with the school counselor, I discovered that we both held similar sentiments about the school. Despite our apartment being within walking distance, the school also offered transportation to and from school. God had delivered on all aspects, even the ones I hadn't considered, He took care of. His blessing of peace of mind concerning Erika's safety traveling to, from, and at school he had sheltered me with. *Once again, God nailed it!*

Elated, I drove to Killeen to communicate the good news to my cousin. "Hey, Carolyn, I found an apartment in Austin, and it's super nice! The vibe of the area aligns with what I envisioned when embarking on my search."

Carolyn couldn't contain her delight. "What an accomplishment! And it all happened before sundown!"

Carolyn, a devout Seventh Day Adventist, observed the Sabbath diligently by refraining from all business-related matters by Friday at sundown and not resume them until Saturday at sundown. Since she had extended such a kind invitation to me, I wanted to comply with her rules and honor her faith.

Once I settled myself in for the evening, I phoned my mother to boast about my success. "Mamma, guess what?"

"What?"

"I found an apartment in Austin!"

"That's great! How much is it?"

"It's $575.00 a month."

At that time, rent of $575.00 was beyond my budget, exceeding what I had paid in San Jose. However, my Austin apartment did have additional amenities. My only income was my unemployment benefits, which were more than the minimum wage and reflected California's cost of living. Compared to today, rent of $575.00 per month would be deemed a monumental bargain.

"What? That's more than your rent in San Jose! Girl, you better find another option. That's too much!" she proclaimed.

Disappointed in my mother's reaction, the next day, I returned to Austin to see if I could find a different apartment. While driving around in Austin, I heard God's soft and calm voice, *What are you doing?*

I spoke aloud to myself. "I'm searching for a more affordable apartment."

But I have already unveiled a place for you to live.

"Yeah, You did." I agreed.

Then, what are you doing?

"Well, Mamma thinks that that apartment is too expensive, so I'm looking for something cheaper."

Don't you think that if I presented you with a place to live, I would also give you the means to afford it?

"Ummm, yeah." I squirmed.

Then, what are you doing?

I pondered my conversation with God and concluded that I should have my head examined, prompting my return to Killeen. I listened, as my mom had advised, but I understood what God had placed on my heart in convincing me that I should trust Him. He whispered in my ear; *Your mom is one of my most faithful and beloved children. She has more faith than many, and I love her always. But her relationship with Me isn't your relationship with Me. They are two separate relationships. And I want you to write or record this in the center of your heart. What I do for her and what I do for you may or may not be the same. It's not that one relationship is better than the other, they are just different. My relationship with each of you is unique.*

And with that, I felt at peace about the apartment that God had selected for me. I relished the remaining part of my trip with Carolyn before taking a flight to San Jose to get ready for my upcoming move.

A month later, I stood in my living room in San Jose, surrounded by the contents of my house all organized and boxed up. The telephone rang, and a lady from an accounting firm, where I had previously interviewed for a job, extended an offer for me to join their organization as an accountant. In my mind, my time in California had concluded. Her offer didn't even tempt me to stay, despite it being at a higher salary than I had earned throughout my entire time in California. If it had been several months earlier, I might have accepted the job. However, with all my belongings now condensed into a single room, I declined her offer.

Because I chose to commence my adventure during the summer season, I flew Erika to New Orleans to stay with my mother while I traveled. Uncertain about what lay ahead, I thought that it would be safer for her to be with my mother. Tears streamed down my face as I bid farewell to San Jose, positive that San Jose now lay in my past and that God alone knew how he would usher all that He had waiting for me in Austin into my life.

I left San Jose on August 15, 1996, in a Ford Tempo, to which I had hitched a 2000-pound U-Haul trailer. I carried all of my earthly belongings, bound for Austin, Texas. Apart from Erika's bed and dresser, my cargo was comprised of clothing, plants, dishes, pots and pans, a select few sentimental items, and my cherished pet bird, Manny.

After bidding farewell to my downstairs neighbors and another friend who came to see me off, I drove away from San Jose with a heavy heart. I drove to Stockton, California, where I picked up my friend, Suzanne. She had agreed to accompany me to Austin on the condition that I would arrange for her return flight to Stockton and give her one hundred dollars for pocket change during our trip.

To this day, I have immense appreciation for Suzanne. She played a crucial role in my relocation, and without her, I don't know how I would have managed. The expedition went well, despite our plans taking an unexpected twist. Because Suzanne did not have great vision, our strategy dictated that she drove during the daylight hours, while I took the wheel at night.

But God had other plans. We stopped to see a friend of hers in Southern California and refreshed ourselves before proceeding to Texas. We pulled out of her friend's house, and she decided that she wanted to drive. So, she drove at night, and I drove during the day.

We drove until we reached El Paso, Texas, where we opted to rest and acknowledged that checking into a hotel would be in our best interests. Besides, the Texas skies were as dark as I had ever seen them.

A notable point in our quest occurred when we stopped at a gas station because the Tempo's transmission had begun to run sluggishly. We presumed that the transmission required fluid, so we sought out a gas station to buy a funnel. Although we had bought half a case of transmission fluid in preparation for our road trip, we overlooked buying a funnel to pour the transmission fluid into the car. The first gas station at which we stopped earned from us the moniker of The Gas Station From

Hell, given that every pump sported an Out Of Order sign, and the dim interior featured a swinging light reminiscent of those in old western movies.

I crept into the musty-smelling shack and observed a 35 to 40-year-old man leaning back in his chair with his feet propped up on the counter, chewing on what I thought to be tobacco.

"Hi, sir, would you happen to have a funnel?"

Without repositioning his body, he drawled with a deep Southern twang, "We ain't got no funnel hea."

My eyes bugged out, and I backed out of the door. "Okay, thanks."

I dashed to the car, jumped in, and belted out, "Girl, this is The Gas Station From Hell because there is no gas, the guy in the store is super spooky, there is no funnel, and the lights are dim as hell inside! What kind of gas station doesn't have a funnel?"

We hightailed it out of that gas station and cruised for a block, which led us to a stop sign. The stop sign sat in pure darkness with not even a hint of light to the left or right of it.

"Man, this kind of darkness makes clear what God intended in Genesis 1:2 when He described the earth as being without form and void and darkness being on the face of the deep. I guess that this is what in the middle of nowhere looks like!" Suzanne chuckled as she kept her eyes on the road and turned right.

Two blocks up the road, surrounded by light, sat an Exxon station. We praised God for finding the Exxon for us, and as an unspoken reward, we bought a few snacks and the funnel. After pouring the transmission fluid into the car, we drove to the nearest hotel.

The next morning, I drove. All rested and eager to be in Austin, we sailed down the road, stopping for the bare necessities such as food, gas, and bathroom breaks. And even at that, it felt like it took forever to drive from El Paso to Austin. It didn't feel like it took us eight and half to nine hours to drive between El Paso and Austin as suggested by Google; it felt more like twelve hours. Google may not have factored in the unexpected detours by road construction and us going the wrong way. Nonetheless, we rolled up on the street of my new home in Austin, Texas, on August 17, 1996. According to Google Maps, it takes twenty-two to twenty-five hours to travel from San Jose to Austin. We made good time when considering that we visited Suzanne's friend in Southern California for five or six hours and we stopped in El Paso to sleep for about seven or eight hours. Driving up to my new home within forty-eight hours after leaving my old home wasn't bad for two ladies who had no idea about driving such a long distance.

In the dark, as fatigued as we were, we grabbed Manny and our suitcases and opted to unhitch and unpack the U-Haul the next morning. We entered the cottage, noticing that the lights were already on, but, alas, the gas remained off. Compelled to take cold showers because the water heater relied on gas, we were surprised to find the cold water refreshing. The heat persisted from earlier in the day, enveloping the cottage in a lingering warmth that made the cold water comfortable and soothing. After showering, Suzanne and I reminisced about our adventure until we fell asleep.

We awoke early the next morning, ready for the day. We unpacked the U-Haul trailer and placed each box in the designated room for unpacking. Then we left to drive to the airport. On the way, we dropped the hitched trailer off at the closest U-Haul store and drove to the Robert Mueller Municipal Airport.

All the way to the airport, thoughts of my impending loneliness after Suzanne left occupied my mind. I disliked parting ways with her, yet I recognized that our destinies led us in different directions and that separate paths had become inevitable. While I had hoped for a lasting relationship with her, our purposes in one another's lives had been accomplished.

God planned for us to help one another, her driving with me to Texas so that I wouldn't have to make the trip alone and me helping her see some of the world outside of Stockton, California. I'm sure that she hasn't forgotten her experience, and I am certain that I will never forget mine. She did call and let me know that she made it home safe and sound.

After seeing Suzanne off, I returned home and unpacked. I didn't have a lot to unpack because I hadn't brought much with me. I did most of my unpacking in the kitchen. The living room and the kitchen separated the two bedrooms and the two bathrooms, leaving some privacy for both Erika and me. A front door led to the front of the apartment, and a back door led to the parking lot. I also had a front porch as well as a back patio. I liked the apartment, and I knew that this move would launch a new life for both Erika and me.

While unpacking and organizing my kitchen cabinets, I found a marijuana joint in one of the cabinets. During that time in my life, I welcomed it. I considered it a housewarming gift that had been selected and left for me by an unknown secret person. I set it aside for later.

Before sunset, I finished my work. I had washed and lined all of the cabinets, sanitized and decorated the bathrooms, and set up Erika's bedroom. Though her bed remained disassembled, I lined her dresser drawers and filled it with her clothes.

In the living room, I laid out the two black bean bag chairs that I had purchased. I decorated the room with plants and flowers. I placed my television on a crate the size of an end table and positioned Manny by the window that overlooked the patio.

I then drove to the grocery store around the corner. I purchased a package of pork chops, some potatoes, various vegetables, drinks, and a few snacks. I returned home after my shopping spree.

Not long after cooking and eating my dinner and freshening up, I prepared to recline, unwind, and savor my evening. While browsing through the television channels, I recalled the joint that I had discovered earlier. I scrutinized it before taking a moderate drag and concluded that its origin was typical homegrown weed cultivated in the ground. Given its presence there and uncertain future procurement avenues, I smoked about a quarter of it and saved the rest for another time.

The next morning, I woke up bright and early, ready to tackle the business at hand. I had filed for unemployment in California before I left, but I needed a job. I visited several temporary agencies and submitted applications to different employers.

I explored Austin, absorbing its charm and uniqueness. The city revealed its allure as I drove up and down Interstate Highway 35 and MoPac, otherwise known as Texas State Highway Loop 1, which is a freeway that unveils access to the west side of Austin. Right off MoPac, I discovered Zilker Park, a vast urban oasis celebrated for its diverse recreational offerings and natural allure. Nestled alongside the Colorado River, the park spans more than 350 acres. Noteworthy attractions include Barton Springs Pool, a natural spring-fed swimming pool with a year-round refreshing temperature, and the Zilker Botanical Garden. The Austin Nature & Science Center adds to the park's appeal, making it a hub for various events and festivals.

Exploring further, I encountered the West Lake Hills area off of Highway 360, triggering memories of Saratoga, California, and its rolling hills. If blindfolded, spun around, and positioned within the West Lake Hills vicinity, I would have sworn that I stood in Saratoga, California. I marveled at the sight as I gazed into the valley at houses perched on hilltops, enveloped by trees, shrubs, flowers, and the glory of nature. It left me breathless!

After soaking it all in, I drove home to my quiet, quaint cottage-style apartment. While driving, a sense of contentment washed over me, because I felt aligned with what I considered God's plan for me to be. I knew that this had to be the land of milk and honey that God had promised me prior to leaving San Jose. Every aspect mirrored a dream that I once had about the destination that God intended for me. The character and feeling of my new home coincided with what He had revealed in that dream.

With the enchanting trees and a serene tranquility that defied description, I couldn't articulate it in words, but my spirit recognized this place to be divinely chosen for me by God.

After being in Austin for a week, I received a letter from the State of California Employment Development Department denying my claim for unemployment insurance benefits. The denial of my claim pointed to the fact that, over the two days of me traveling from San Jose to Austin, I had neglected to actively pursue employment, a prerequisite for eligibility to receive unemployment insurance benefits.

This appeared to be the most absurd thing that I had ever encountered! How could I search for employment in a place where I had no intention of residing? The correspondence specified that to contest the decision, I must contact a designated number and arrange a hearing. On the scheduled hearing date, I positioned myself by the telephone, awaiting the call that would grant me the chance to communicate to someone in the State of California the sheer absurdity of denying my claim. Finally, the phone rang.

"Hello, yes, is this Vivian Thomas?" A man with a deep voice bellowed.

"Yes, it is."

"I'm from the State of California Employment Development Department, and I'm calling to conduct a hearing for a claim to receive unemployment insurance benefits that was initially denied."

"Yes, sir."

The man explained the process and afterwards swore me in, which was standard protocol for hearing proceedings.

"Miss Thomas, can you give me your reason for not seeking employment on the dates of August 16th and 17th of 1996?"

"Yes, sir, on those dates, I moved from California to Austin, Texas. I did not seek employment on those dates because I was driving to Austin from San Jose. Also, seeking employment in California, a place from where I had moved, would have been nonsensical."

"Is this a permanent relocation to Austin, Texas?"

"Yes, sir."

"Okay, Miss Thomas, that is all the questions that I have. A determination of this appeal will be mailed to you within two weeks. Thank you for your time."

I put down the phone, flabbergasted at what had transpired. He had not even given me a moment to convey to him the absurdity of it all. Inconceivable!

By the end of the first week, I received a determination that the State of California would compensate me with unemployment insurance benefits at $7.00 per hour, a favorable outcome as the minimum wage at that time was $5.35 per hour. Once more, God had come through for me. A week after receiving the determination that I would receive unemployment insurance benefits from the State of California, my mom suggested that I apply for food stamps.

"What, apply for food stamps?" I strenuously objected.

There's no way that I'm applying for food stamps. My upbringing did not include applying for food stamps! I had received government assistance through Aid to Families with Dependent Children (AFDC) before moving to California, but that was the limit of my willingness to accept government assistance. *No food stamps!*

"Yes, and what's wrong with applying for food stamps? That's your money. You've paid for it with the taxes that you pay. It won't hurt you to apply. That will be one less thing that you'll have to worry about," My mom persuasively chimed in.

I sighed. "Yeah, well, I'll think about it."

Later that night, I heard God during my prayer time. *Why don't you want to apply for food stamps?*

"Well, I don't want to go on food stamps. That's not my M-O. I don't want a handout like food stamps. Besides, it's been my experience when dealing with government workers who administer those kinds of programs that they treat folks seeking food stamps like lowlifes, and they make those who apply for these kinds of benefits wait around as if their time doesn't matter."

So, is that pride that I'm detecting?

I was shocked! "Pride? Oh, no, that's not pride. I don't want you to think that I'm being prideful, so I'll apply tomorrow."

The next morning, determined not to confront God on the issue of pride, I planned to visit the food stamp office. From my observations, people who God dealt with regarding pride ended up going through hell, and I didn't want that for myself. That heartache would be an unnecessary heartache.

God needed no further communication to guide me toward my apparent objective. I entered the food stamp office dressed in business attire, with all essential paperwork in my briefcase. After a fifteen-minute wait, a lady called my name. It surprised me when she called my name because I had assumed that I would be there for at least an hour before being helped. I proceeded to her office, responded to all of her questions, and supplied all of the paperwork that she requested.

Once the meeting concluded, the lady instructed me to wait in the lobby while she created a food stamp card for me. In less than thirty minutes, my business with the food stamp office had been conducted and completed. I drove out of the parking lot amazed and impressed. It was mind-blowing how fast the process had gone for me.

In talking to two or three people as I waited, I discovered that they had been sitting there for two or three hours prior to me walking through the door, the very nightmare that had made me not want to apply for food stamps. But God intervened, and I didn't have the long wait that others evidently had, nor did I experience disrespectful treatment by the workers. This let me know that God heard and understood my hesitation regarding applying for food stamps. It proved to me that He does hear and listen to me.

Regarding the amount I received in food stamps, I had never eaten better! I received $218.00 per month for Erika and me, which was enough to purchase more than enough food for both of us. We ate like the rich and famous: specialty items, seafood, fresh vegetables, organic foods... you name it, we ate it.

I had been in Austin for three weeks, and the school year had crept up upon us. In September of 1996, my parents and my aunt drove Erika to Austin from New Orleans. While visiting, my dad helped me set up Erika's bed.

In my bedroom, I had a twin mattress, which Will's mother had loaned me, and a rocking chair. Our neighbor Will was a year older than Erika, and he attended the same school as she did.

Will's parents and I took responsibility for making sure that both Erika and Will had rides to and from school activities. Will's parents and I held the same sentiments when it came to ensuring our children's safe transportation. Will and his family proved to be neighbors upon whom I could depend. And now, Will has become my unofficially adopted son.

I also had in my room a homemade cardboard dresser with doors and a shelf in it. My mom and aunt couldn't laugh hard enough at my cardboard dresser. To this day, my mom laughs when reminiscing about my cardboard dresser.

Six months after their visit, I returned the items that Will's mother had loaned to me because I purchased a queen-size bed. But I still didn't have a dresser. I had also purchased a washer and dryer because the laundry mat wore on me, both in terms of time and in terms of money.

By November of 1996, concerns lingered because I hadn't secured permanent employment. I accepted several assignments from temporary agencies, yet permanent opportunities with benefits remained elusive. The Lord knew our need for benefits, but He reassured me that I should not fret. With clear guidance, He comforted me with an assurance that once I secured employment, it would be long-term, so I should relish my time off. Following His counsel, I relaxed in contentment.

He instructed me to rise early each morning, the same way that I would if I had a job. He wanted me to exercise and keep my place clean and organized because disorganization can show up in subtle (or not so subtle) ways during a job interview. For example, due to disorganization, a person may illustrate disorganized thought processes; a person can give inconsistent, vague, or rambling answers; they can present poor time awareness by being late for the interview or by not being mindful of time limits; and/or they may prove to be unprepared by speaking unclearly or simply fumbling papers. God wanted me to keep my mind sharp and organized instead of dull-minded and idle. So, every morning, after Erika left for school, I ran a mile around the neighborhood trail, cleaned and vacuumed my apartment, and cooked dinner for Erika. By the time that Erika returned home from school, greens, red beans, cornbread, shrimp fried rice, and whatever else I cooked could be smelled from a block away.

In the early part of November of 1996, I received a letter from the Food Stamp Administration stating that my food stamp benefits would be cut to $36.00 per month and that on November 18, 1996, I needed to reapply, attend a short presentation, and submit documentation showing that I could not seek education and/or training. The letter stated that failure to do so might jeopardize my food stamp benefits.

After reading the letter, I closed my eyes and spoke to God. "Well, Lord, You must have a job for me because You know that $36.00 is not enough to sustain us."

On November 18, 1996, I entered the office to which the letter instructed me to go. I attended the presentation and submitted the documentation that reflected the fact that I was receiving unemployment insurance benefits from the State of California and was obligated to seek employment which prevented me from dedicating time for training and pursuit of educational courses. Moreover, since I already had a bachelor's degree and several years of work experience, I didn't need further education or training. I needed a job.

After the representative reviewed my documentation, she instructed me to wait in the lobby until my name was called.

While waiting in the lobby, the chairs beside me filled up. As the line for assistance grew longer and longer, I noticed this guy standing in line tucking his shirt into his pants. He reminded me of Jethro Bodine from the Beverly Hillbillies. He appeared attractive yet somewhat folksy.

He glanced in my direction, but this didn't register at the time. I had not even thought of meeting someone in ages. My entire focus centered on ensuring that I had the means to sustain food for my household.

I never saw him approach me, but before I knew it, he sat down beside me.

He opened the conversation in a calm, polite voice. "Hi, what's your name? Do you mind if I take this seat?"

"Viv, and no, I don't mind."

"Where are you from? You don't sound like you're from around here." He settled comfortably into the seat next to me.

"I'm not. I'm from New Orleans by way of San Jose, California."

"Yeah, you sounded like you had an unfamiliar accent. I've just gotten out."

I didn't know what that meant, but I assumed he meant the hospital or clinic because he walked with a limp signifying that he had a recent injury. For some reason, it didn't occur to me to ask him to clarify.

"Yeah, I broke my heel." He bent over to rub his heel.

"Wow, how did you do that?"

"I jumped over a fence and landed on it wrong."

I flinched. "Oh, man, that had to hurt."

"Yeah, well, it's not so bad. So, do you have a husband or a significant other in your life?"

"No, not right now."

"Why don't you have a man in your life? Never mind, I know why."

I was gobsmacked. "Oh, really? Why?"

"Because you're waiting on God to send you the right man."

At that moment my spirit became attached to his spirit. I could just feel it. I didn't know what it meant, but I felt it! I cannot explain what it felt like. Somehow, I just knew.

I sputtered, my hands shaking, "You know, you might just be right."

He stuck his hand out to shake my hand. "By the way, I'm Terry Martin."

"Hello, Terry Martin, it's nice to meet you."

"Well, I'm going to be on my way in a minute, but before I leave, can I have your phone number?"

"Ummm..."

He cut me off. "You know, here's my number. Call me if you want to talk sometime."

He wrote his number down and handed it to me. I figured that his offering his number to me rather than waiting for me to give him mine was a strategy that he used to avoid rejection.

I took his number. "Okay."

He left. I felt amazed, yet sort of dumbstruck when I realized that all of the people sitting in the rows of chairs and standing in line had also left.

Wow, what a personable and friendly man. His spirit felt so at ease and so pleasant. He spoke with me as if he had known me all his life. Wow!

Not long after he left a lady called my name, my business was concluded, and I drove home. I thought about Terry Martin all the way home. It had been a long time since I had entertained the thought of dating or even having male companionship. After changing my clothes and making myself comfortable at home, I cooked dinner, waited for Erika to get home from school at 3:30, and helped her with her homework. At 7:00 p.m., Erika and I ate dinner and relaxed for the rest of the evening.

While lying on the couch, I found myself replaying my conversation with Terry over and over in my head. That's when I decided to call him.

At 8:00, I retired to my room and dialed his number. "Hello, may I speak with Terry?"

"Who's calling?" a soft, loving voice mumbled.

I later learned that his mother had answered the phone.

"This is Vivian."

"Oh, hold on one minute, please." She laid the receiver down.

Terry picked up the phone. "Hello, this is Terry."

"Hi, this is Viv. How are you doing?"

"Oh, hi, I'm fine, how are you?

After casual conversation about the weather, I moved on to one of the questions that I like to ask to determine how well a person knows themselves and how truthful they are willing to be.

I proceeded with my question. "What do you like least about yourself?"

He guffawed. "Being inconsistent!"

"What do you mean?"

"You know, I do well for a while, and then I regress. I can't seem to maintain consistency. I'm always falling off."

"Well, I think that we all do that from time to time," I retorted.

"Yeah, but it always happens to me."

"What does it mean to fall off? Fall off of what?"

"Well, to be honest, I smoke crack. I tried quitting, but I keep going back to it. I recently spent six months in jail. While in jail, I prayed to God for help, and soon after being released, He sent me you. You're my help."

I sat there in silence, searching for the right words. I didn't want to hurt his feelings because my spirit had connected with his spirit. Somehow, I felt that I knew his spirit. I knew him. It's like God gave me insight that went beyond his being, into his spirit, and pierce his soul, which is where He revealed to my spirit what Terry needed most. It felt as though we had known each other in another life, and I recognized him, what he needed, and his capabilities. I listened to him as he described his battle with drug addiction, his upbringing, his parents, his siblings, his children, his first marriage and divorce, and the jobs that he had worked.

When he finished speaking, I told him about myself, my daughter, my parents, my siblings, my upbringing, my moves to California and Austin. I assured him that I was not the kind of person who thinks unkindly of others, nor did I pass judgment on others, because every human being has shortcomings and need God's help to overcome them. There is not one of us who should think that he or she is better than another person.

He communicated his sentiments regarding God and said that he knew that one day God would help him overcome his drug addiction. By the end of our conversation, we had discovered so much about each other and decided that our meeting had indeed been a part of God's divine plan for our lives, so we agreed to see one another soon.

And without my realizing it, three hours had passed. I lay in bed thinking about our conversation. He had a familiar heart. It made me think about my three friends who battled crack cocaine addiction detailed in previous chapters. I saw the three of them within Terry. He had a loving, kind, and protective spirit like Bill, a sense of humor like Chico, and the generous heart of Lylah.

Over the next week, Terry and I conversed, and I found tremendous pleasure in hearing about his desires, his dreams, his aspirations, and his downfalls. However, my initial reaction led me to what my pre-conceived notions were and my own experiences with drug addicts, and I immediately felt reluctance. I recalled having to endure being lied to, stolen from, and having to watch the destruction of a person I loved. *God, no! A drug addict? You've got to be kidding me.* I liked Terry and thought that he was a nice guy, but upon remembering about the lives of my friends, the difficulties that they faced, and the stories that I witnessed and heard from others, my support for Terry and his drug addiction became overshadowed by thoughts of the hardships that we might face in the future.

God heard my refusal to involve myself with Terry's issues. *Okay, you can deal with this now or later. I suggest that you deal with it now while you're in your early thirties because it will take a lot more when you're in your forties and fifties. People's energy levels tend to reduce as they age, you know. It's up to you. I am doing a new thing.* In other words, I'm taking an approach to which he is not accustomed.

I finally called Stacey to obtain her opinion on what I had heard from God.

"Well, it sounds like He has spoken. And you know, you better do whatever He places on your heart." Stacey's wisdom won the day.

I agreed. I didn't realize it then, but the fact that I didn't want to deal with Terry's issues should have been a tell-tale sign that God Himself had spoken to my spirit because most of the time, my flesh pushed against me following the direction in which God wanted me to go.

The fact that Terry possessed all of the best qualities of the friends about whom I've written in this book also hinted at God's involvement and intentions for me to walk in the direction of dealing with Terry's drug addiction. Though neglected as a thought from the onset of His guidance, I'm convinced that God used my friends' lives and situations to equip me to handle Terry's tribulations by acquainting me with the characteristics of drug addiction. This enabled me to break through the prejudices that clouded my perceptions after hearing of Terry's drug addiction.

Through prolonged contemplation, He enabled me to see that the behaviors of lying, stealing, and inconsistencies can manifest even in good-hearted individuals, courtesy of the nature of drug addiction, not the character of the person facing it. He taught me to look beyond the faults and discern the underlying needs crying out to be addressed.

Terry and I talked every night for the next week. And then three days before Thanksgiving, I received a call from the City of Austin's Compensation Manager, who invited me to interview for a temporary position in their Human Resources Compensation Division. Bursting with pure joy, I accepted the invitation.

I called both my mom and Terry to announce my good news about my upcoming interview. They both wished me well and offered me encouraging, uplifting words. They both stated that they felt that I would do well in the interview and hoped that I would be hired for the job.

The night before my interview, Terry and I talked on the phone until after midnight, even though I had to rise early the next morning. This did not bother me because staying up late and functioning on limited sleep seemed to be no major deal for me.

The following morning, I jumped up, dressed, saw Erika off to school, and raced off to my interview. Two ladies interviewed me, both seemed anxious about meeting me and discovering what I brought to the table.

They offered me a seat and some water. During our conversation, one of the ladies informed me that my resume had been floating around the city and had landed on her desk. She articulated that my qualifications had impressed her, and she had passed along my resume to the other lady, who suggested calling me in for an interview.

After fifteen minutes of conversation with the two women, wherein I answered ten or more questions, one lady stated that, after meeting with me, she felt that I would be an excellent addition to their organization. The other lady agreed and offered me the job right on the spot! I thanked both of them and exerted every ounce of the strength that I possessed to refrain from leaping in the air out of exhilaration.

I couldn't wait to call my mom and Terry to let them know that I had been offered the job and that my hire date would be on December 2, 1996. As soon as I returned home, I called my mom. After that I helped Erika with her homework, and then I called Terry.

I had hoped that Terry would spend the Thanksgiving weekend with us, but he couldn't because he attended the anniversary of the National Gospel Announcers Guild Association ceremony with his parents and his sisters in Houston, Texas. So, I spent that Thanksgiving with Erika and Will.

I had the good fortune of meeting my neighbor, Elaine, who lived in the cottage next to mine. We walked around the neighborhood trail two or three times a week. On that Thanksgiving, we spent time together, articulating our gratitude for the blessings that God had granted us.

I broadcast my good news to her about my new job and the guy I had met. She had heard of his family but had no acquaintance with them. Terry's dad, Bill Martin, had a notable reputation in the community as a gospel radio announcer, a fact unbeknownst to me upon meeting Terry. Some folks in the community referred to him as *the mailman*, but I thought that this nickname stemmed from his role as a mailman for the U.S. Postal Service. However, I later discovered that *the mailman* referred to his radio handle.

As the months passed and Terry and I grew closer, his addiction manifested when he disappeared for long periods of time, which reminded me of the times when Chico vanished for weeks at a time. I never knew when he would withdraw. The first time, I didn't hear from

Terry for a week. Upon resurfacing, his explanation for his disappearing act involved him visiting his brother's house and losing track of time.

In the early part of 1997, while working at the airport, which was just around the corner from his dad's house at the time, I permitted Terry to borrow my car. At the end of my day, I requested that one of the airport police officers drop me off at Terry's dad's house. I waited for hours, and Terry never showed up, so his dad offered to take me home. Terry did not return with my car until the next morning; and as luck and God's blessings would have it, that day happened to be one of my scheduled days off.

The term *pissed off* did not do justice to the extent of my anger, but by the time Terry showed up at my house with my car, I had managed to calm down. Upon seeing Terry that morning, I embraced him, advised him to take a shower, and then instructed him to go to bed. I surprised myself because under normal circumstances, I would have ripped a hole in his behind!

Elaine helped me navigate my fury, and our friendship was invaluable to me. God used Elaine as one of those anchors about which I spoke earlier. In moments of extreme ire, I conversed with her, and her thoughtful responses had a calming effect on my spirit, bringing relief to my mind and soul. And I am grateful that she played such a significant role in my life. Although I may not have been conscious of it, I needed her in ways that I couldn't even fathom.

Reflecting on my life then, I didn't have a clue what the outcome would be, nor did I know what it all meant or would mean. I had no idea, nor had I ever read anything about the experiences and adventures awaiting me.

I had learned about God, Jesus, and the Holy Spirit, but my full identity in Christ, the nature of the enemy or the forces of evil, and their impact on me, I remained immature.

> *The thief comes only to steal and kill and destroy; I have come that they may have life and have it to the full.*
> John 10:10 (NIV).

The thief in this scripture represents the evil or the enemy. It is this enemy that I consider to be my enemy, and this enemy is often referred to as the devil, Satan, or the evil one.

Up until this point in my life, my experiences had been minimal as they related to the Holy Spirit and the spirit world. From this point on, however, the lessons that I had already learned and that I would learn speak to the events through which I lived, and lessons taught by God Himself.

By this point, God had delivered on His promises to me that I would have a home, a man, and a job. And with these provisions, I was positioned to learn and focus on the lessons, complications, hurdles, and trials that I would have to face. In addition, learning my identify in Christ, the power that I possessed through Christ, and the power that I have over the enemy also materialized and became more evident.

CHAPTER EIGHT

THE FINAL PREPARATIONS

To crush the enemy, I must first know who my enemy is. Sun Tzu's *The Art of War* states, *If you know neither your enemy nor yourself, you will succumb in every battle.* So, it was imperative that I acquaint myself with my identity in Christ and the enemy that fights against me.

In October of 1998, I completed a workbook entitled *The Making of a Warrior: A Tool For Living A Victorious Life* by Rodney D. Walker that I purchased from a church function. In a recent online search for this workbook, I could not find it. However, in this book the author teaches us how to be a worshipping warrior, how to walk with God, how the enemy works, and furnishes enlightenment on the authority that Christians have through Jesus. I used this book, along with scriptures in the Bible and prayer, as a resource for preparing me for spiritual warfare and enhancing my worship life.

Raised as someone who regularly took part in church services, my loss of interest in church alarmed me. It stirred in me emotions of a backslider or someone who had forsaken their commitment to partaking in church services.

I cried out to God, "Lord! Satan is trying to keep me from going to church. I need your help to overcome him!"

God heard me. *That is not Satan. For to what I'm about to make known to you, I need your undivided attention. I don't need you to be distracted by the lady wearing the nice hat or the cute baby with the fat face. I need all of your attention and focus.*

Wow! I had never had that happen to me before. But I understood what He meant. I understood that the lessons in my future had to be taught by Him alone and in isolation.

One night while watching one of the TV ministries, a pastor of a megachurch, who I had never heard of, had an altar call. An altar call is a tradition in many Christian churches, particularly evangelical and charismatic denominations, where the pastor or minister encourages individuals to come forward to the altar for prayer, to re-dedicate their life to Jesus Christ, and/or to become a member of the church. The altar call is often accompanied by a call to repentance and an offer to receive salvation or other spiritual blessings. That night, droves of people flocked to the altar.

At the altar, a woman addressed the minister directly, explaining that her presence wasn't solely for herself but also for her brother. She pronounced her intention to stand in intercessory prayer for her brother, whose drug addiction had escalated and who needed delivery from it.

This caught my attention. The pastor joined hands with the woman and requested that the audience, as well as his television family, join him in prayer. I stood and lifted my hands to the Lord to participate in the prayer. As the pastor prayed, a forceful energy thrust me against the wall, and a growling, unrecognizable sound burst out of my mouth as if a wild animal had been loosed. That same energy pinned me to the wall for a few seconds before I collapsed to the floor. After assimilating the situation, I crawled into bed, the last action of which I had memory. After what felt like only a moment in time, the sun woke me up.

I stuttered as I got out of bed. "Lord, what happened?"

I had to remove the spirit of fear.

Oh, my God, the spirit of fear felt like a monstrous force unwilling to be evicted from my person. Yet, God felt that drawing it out took precedence over the rest of His plan. After contemplating His words, they made sense because the spirit of fear, by its very nature, was a negative force that could oppose my faith, courage, and trust in God. This negative force could have affected my emotions, thoughts, and actions, thereby debilitating me and preventing me from accomplishing God's plan. Removing the fear first would also give me the control that I needed to stand and conquer whatever power the enemy would attempt to exert over me.

> *...for God has not given us a spirit of fear, but of power and of love and of a sound mind.*
>
> 2 Timothy 1:7 (NKJV)

God had to banish the fear because I hadn't gotten it from Him in the first place.

God cannot lie, so to stay true to His Word, he eliminated my fear and replaced it with power, love, and a sound mind. What an extraordinary God and an awesome experience!

When I walked with Elaine that evening, I relayed to her the events that had unfolded, and she assumed the role that God had intended for her in my life. As I spoke, she listened and voiced a sense of astonishment similar to mine.

And just to check my sanity, I called my faithful spiritual advisor, Stacey. "You'll never guess what happened." So, I filled her in on all that had occurred.

Stacey proclaimed, "Well, in my opinion, this is the inception point, and I'm confident that over time, it will become even more intriguing and quite captivating..."

"Yeah, you're probably right."

Later that night, as I sat on my bed, I noticed a dark cloud hovering in the corner between the ceiling and the wall. Somehow, I knew that the enemy was present there, and at that moment the enemy pinned me to the bed.

Without an ounce of fear, I screamed, "Jesus!"

The moment that I called Jesus's name; the force of the enemy subsided and released me from the bed. I always had the assurance that I could reach out to Jesus and that He would be there, but this instance felt different. He did not delay. He showed up at that very moment! I encountered the power of Jesus in a manner unprecedented to me.

Even as I deemed the day's experience sufficient, God had one more phenomenon for me to witness, an exchange between my spirit and the enemy.

The enemy declared, "You can't cast me out. You smoke cigarettes."

My spirit retorted, "So, what? Paul had an infirmity, and he cast you out."

The enemy departed without delay. God revealed yet another lesson to me: to wield His Word, for it renders the enemy powerless.

> *...because He who is in you is greater than he who is in the world.*
> 1 John 4:4 (NKJV)

The spirit within me is the me that God chose before He even created the world.

> *Just as He chose us in Him before the foundation of the world, that we should be holy and without blame before Him in love.*
> Ephesians 1:4 (NKJV).

God created my spirit from his own image before He created the world, so He knows better than any living soul all that I am. He knows what I'm capable of and what I am not capable of. All that He required of me had already been placed in me, however, grasping and employing what already resided within me presented complication and great contemplation for me.

To teach me how to utilize the gifts that He had conferred upon me, God and I spent hours every day in His Word. I talked with Him, and He talked to me in my heart, my mind, and through His Word. He used ministers and everyday people to confirm ideas, perspectives, directions, comprehension, and a whole host of affirmations that He knew I needed to advance in my faith. He blessed me with dreams and visions. He even interpreted those dreams and visions so that I could apprehend their meaning and so that I could comprehend the power of God and the authority that He bestowed upon me.

One vision that He brought to me unfolded as Terry and I attended a Mighty Clouds of Joy concert at the University of Texas. His dad acted as the Master of Ceremonies. While his dad entertained the audience before the first opening sequence, Terry left the auditorium to take his nieces and nephews to the bathroom.

During his absence, I sat in the audience, next to Terry's brother. But for six seconds, instead of seeing his dad, I saw Terry on stage acting as the Master of Ceremonies.

When his dad reappeared on the stage, I tapped Terry's brother's arm and whispered in his ear, "Did you see that?"

"See what?"

I pointed to the stage. "Terry. Up on the stage."

"Girl, you're crazy. Terry's not on the stage."

I searched around me to see if I saw Terry and the kids, but they were nowhere in sight.

Upon Terry's return, I pulled him to me and pointed towards the stage, "Were you on stage?"

Pointing in the direction of the stage, "On stage?"

"Yes."

"No, why?"

"I thought that I saw you up there instead of your dad."

"No, you didn't see me."

I knew, without a shadow of a doubt, that I had seen Terry on that stage. For the rest of the night, the thought of seeing Terry on the stage lingered in my mind while we mingled backstage with members of the Mighty Clouds of Joy.

On the ride home from the concert, while Terry and I talked about how much we liked the concert, I heard God utter to my spirit that He had shown me the end result in the vision that I saw on the stage. I didn't know what He meant. I presumed that He meant that He had shown me a glimpse of Terry's future.

I didn't mention the vision or what God had spoken to me on the drive home. I left that matter between God and me for years before conversing with a single soul about it. I think that I didn't communicate anything to others about the vision because I didn't know what it meant. I didn't know if the vision meant that Terry would become a Master of Ceremonies, or if following in his father's footsteps as a radio announcer was his future, or if speaking in front of large audiences would become his destiny. Or if any of that or none of that would be his plight. I just didn't know.

The other reason is that I didn't want what God had shown me to be messed up or jinxed by the enemy. As if the enemy could mess up God's plan, but at the time, the thought crossed my mind. And I also suspect that I kept it to myself because I didn't want to be thought of as delusional by others who had not seen the vision.

Some of the visions and dreams that I've had over my lifetime have materialized and some have not, well, at least not yet. I have learned from observing others who have had dreams and visions and from reading God's Word that some dreams and visions may manifest quickly while others may take years to actualize. But I stand steadfast on that within the deepest recesses of my soul that my dreams and visions from God will manifest, in God's own time and for His own purposes.

As God prepared me to take on the assignment of helping my husband overcome his drug addiction, He implemented several avenues of preparing me for the task. Paths such as deepening my faith and relationship with Him through prayer and meditation, offering guidance and wisdom through scriptures, communion with spiritual leaders, internal examination of my own trials, enabling me to have direct contact and fellowship with others who aligned with my convictions for encouragement and support, and giving me peace of mind when needed.

God also prepared me for the task by teaching me lessons through scriptures, sermons, and personal revelations, to which he unveiled and revealed to me. Rodney D. Walker's *The Making of a Warrior: A Tool For Living A Victorious Life* guided me in recognizing and receiving revelation of God's Will and purpose for my life. Mr. Walker's teaching helped to reveal the power that God had instilled in me by my views and reliance on Jesus's sacrifices, which deepened my faith and commitment to Jesus and His plans for me. And through faith, I gained the ability to embrace the spiritual gifts, skills, and resources with which He equipped me to fulfill my calling, to embrace the hope, assurance, and a visualization of the greater purpose in and beyond my life.

He taught me to trust Him and the power that He instilled in me.

> *Most assuredly, I say to you, he who believes in Me, the works that I do he will do also; and greater works than these he will do, because I go to My Father.*
>
> John 14:12 (NKJV)

It's evident that the power that He has granted me usurps any power that the enemy claims to have over me.

He guided me through scripture after scripture, showing me how Jesus cast demons (unclean spirits) out and how when those unclean spirits recognized him, they trembled.

> *Now a large herd of swine was feeding near the mountains. So, all the demons begged Him, saying, "Send us to the swine, that we may enter them." And at once Jesus gave them permission. Then the unclean spirits went out and entered the swine (there were about two thousand); and the herd ran violently down the steep place into the sea and drowned in the sea.*
>
> Mark 5:11-13 (NKJV)

Those unclean spirits knew that they couldn't stay in His presence and that he had authority over them.

I marveled as He revealed the truth about my identity in Christ and the power that he had bestowed upon me as His child, an heir of His Son

Jesus. He called me anointed because of Christ who lives within me and warned the enemy not to touch or harm me because I am one of His.

> *Blessed is the man who walks not in the counsel of the ungodly, nor stands in the path of sinners, nor sits in the seat of the scornful; but his delight is in the law of the Lord, and in His law, he meditates day and night. He shall be like a tree, planted by the rivers of water, that brings forth its fruit in its seasons, whose leaf also shall not wither; and whatever he does shall prosper.*
>
> Psalms 1:1-3 (NKJV)

This scripture was embedded in my heart and instructed me to not do what wicked people told me to do or live a sinful, unremorseful life. Instead, I should study and ponder His words on an ongoing basis so that my faith would be secured, which would produce results that would lead me to prosperity in all that I did.

He poured awareness into me about who He made and declared me to be in Him. The more I read, the more I internalized and declared my identity, which gave me confidence and the boldness that He knew I needed to maintain a sense of control over my life, a certainty of who I am in Christ, and the ability to operate in the power that God had given me to utilize as I pursued God's plans for me.

> *Put on the whole armor of God, that you may be able to stand against the wiles of the devil.*
>
> Ephesians 6:11 (NKJV)

I never understood what Paul meant until I studied the various aspects of the armor of God and until I faced an adversary that required me to make sense of the attire, as well as each intricate detail of the many components that made up the complete outfit. I discovered that each piece played a significant role in spiritual warfare and that utilizing each of them in the appropriate manner was essential in prevailing and achieving a victory.

The Bible identifies what makes up the armor of God.

Stand therefore, having girded your waist with truth, having put on the breastplate of righteousness, and having shod your feet with the preparation of the gospel of peace; above all, taking the shield of faith with which you will be able to quench all the fiery darts of the wicked one. And take the helmet of salvation, and the sword of the Spirit, which is the word of God, praying always with all prayer and supplication in the Spirit, being watchful to this end with all perseverance and supplication for all the saints...

Ephesians 6:14-18 (NKJV)

My perspective of Ephesians 6:14 is that girding my lions with truth, in simple terms, means to know and discern the truth about God, who God is, the power that He possesses, and His relationship to me. And I must know the truth about myself, who I am, as defined by God, and my relationship to God. In addition, I must know the truth about who the enemy is and/or the truth about the forces that work against me. Truths such as that enemies and evil forces have no power over me, and the spirit that lives within me is greater and more powerful than any enemy or force working against me.

Knowing the truth is easier to grasp in concept than it is in actual practice due to the difficulty of knowing and accepting the truth. I have experienced the old adage *the truth hurts* a time or two in my life, but throughout my life I have found that knowing the truth quite often proved to be better than not knowing. Knowing the truth enabled me to solicit God's help through prayer. And what I didn't know, my spirit knew and solicited God's help for me. I knew that avoiding the truth would be accepting a lie and that refusing to address the truth would keep me in a blinded state.

Besides, God encourages and instructs His children to deal with Him in spirit and in truth. Facing and accepting the truth places me in a position for God to help me overcome concerns by giving me the insight necessary to prevail over all obstacles, adversities, and day-to-day problems that I may encounter.

The second aspect of the armor of God in Ephesians 6:14 is the breastplate of righteousness. It symbolizes the protection and virtues necessary for followers of Christ to stand firm against spiritual turmoil. It signifies living in accordance with God's standards and is obtained by being justified or deemed righteous through faith. This righteousness could not be obtained by my works or deeds. Christ alone placed this righteousness upon me through his death and resurrection. But my faith gave me access to it.

For so many years, I had been taught that I had to live by The Ten Commandments listed in the Bible in Exodus 20:1-17 and a reiteration of them by Moses in Deuteronomy 5:4-21. I had learned that breaking any one of them meant that I had sinned and compromised my salvation. But God taught me otherwise. He taught me that because of His grace, if I believed in my heart and confessed with my mouth that Jesus is Lord, I would be saved. This meant that His grace saved me and that there was no deed that I could have performed to be saved. The Bible speaks of numerous people, despite their sinful natures, that God used and exalted. People such as David, who killed a man because he wanted the man's wife for himself, who, even after being punished by God, God referred to him as the apple of His eye. And Paul, who persecuted Jesus and his followers, and after a spiritual transformation that occurred on the road to Damacus, God used him to lead thousands to repentance. These examples are further proof that it's not our works or deeds that saves us, but it is God's grace alone. And this truth set me free and gave me confidence that I had indeed been set free!

The most common weapons that Satan uses against God's people to cause them to stumble or be subdued are doubt, fear, and anxiety. Satan knows that if he can convince people to doubt God, feel fear, and feel anxiety, he stands a chance of overcoming them and that using distractions works well in derailing and sidetracking his prey. Sometimes all it takes to change the course of a person's life is doubt, fear, or anxiety. Satan doesn't have to destroy people to divert someone from his overall goal or purpose.

The thief does not come except to steal, and to kill, and to destroy...
John 10:10 (NKJV)

In this scripture the thief refers to the enemy of one's soul.

The third aspect of the armor of God is for me to wear upon my feet the gospel of peace, which I translated to mean being confident, grounded, and ready to move forward with the assignment given to me in faith, certainty, and peace. I pledged my allegiance to God, the assignment that He had given me, and I committed myself to having a humble demeanor and a peaceful stride that comes from the gospel of Jesus Christ.

One example of this is when I kept my peace, despite the ridicule, confusion, and intrusion of the mission of helping Terry overcome his addiction. Many family members and friends were not knowledgeable or familiar with the assignment that God had given me, perhaps they could not foresee the plans that God had for Terry, but I knew, even when I felt confused, that God had sent me to help where He needed me to. Rather than succumbing to the ridicule, I stood my ground and kept the peace that God had given me through the gospel of Christ.

I recall in the beginning of my assignment that God had given me the ability to find Terry in a city about which I knew nothing, the city of Austin. When Terry left, which I called disappearing for weeks at a time, God led me to him every single time. After a month or two of being led to Terry by God, I earned the dubious distinction, from my mother-in-law, of being the one person in the world who could find Terry.

Upon finding out that Terry had disappeared, my mother-in-law used to become exasperated in the extreme. "Tell Vivian, she'll find him."

We used to laugh about this. After three or four months of being led to him, God placed in my heart that I should no longer pursue him, so I stopped. This disappointed some people, but I had to follow the direction in which God wanted me to go. He put in my spirit that He no longer needed me to track Terry because the purpose of me finding him had been accomplished.

With God's peace upon me, other people's actions and thoughts didn't bother me the way that they would have without it. In fact, God had prevented me from speaking on many occasions, making it impossible for me to become combative or lose my peace, even during times when I wanted to defend my position or tell someone to butt out of my business.

Peace is a constant necessity because peace is a manifestation of faith and trust in God. I knew and relied upon who God had created me to be and in the process of confessing His Word.

> *For as he thinks in his heart, so is he.* Proverbs 23:7 (NKJV)

This scripture protects my peace from being stolen, my confidence from being broken, strife from residing in me, and stopping myself from being crushed or falling short. If I think such negativity, then that will be my faith. Possessing peace is an assurance that God has my back and that He is always working on my behalf. And with that assurance, my peace is secured.

The fourth aspect of the armor of God is taking up the shield of faith, which requires a faith that is beyond simply trusting in God and involves fully depending on Him in every aspect. This level of faith comes from spending time with Him, thanking Him, praising and worshipping Him, seeking His guidance and wisdom, meditating on His Word, and conversing with Him. Whether one realizes it or not, God talks and writes when permitted. Some may wonder how God may not be permitted to talk or write. It's easy. Whenever I'm caught up in my own thoughts and I'm talking so much that I don't stop to listen to God, in essence, I'm preventing Him from communicating in response to what I am saying. And just as my mom said to me years ago, it's no different than that — asking Him a question and failing to wait for an answer.

Many times, when I wrote my thoughts and questions down, I received a response or revelation from God without any further effort on my part. It was as if He seized the pen, with me unaware of His hold on it, while words flowed onto the page, melting into it as the paper absorbed His every direction, concept, and revelation — insights that could not have originated from my own mind or ideas.

> *...in all your ways acknowledge Him, and He shall direct your paths.*
> Proverbs 3:5 (NKJV)

Interacting with God activated my faith, and reliance upon Him exercised my faith. The difference between activating and exercising is that activating my faith involved initiating it, and exercising my faith meant relying upon it and trudging through life's multitude of experiences because of it. Taking up the shield of faith also required me to receive God's Word and all that He spoke to my spirit about it.

> *Now faith is the substance of things hoped for, the evidence of things not seen.*
> Hebrews 11:1 (NKJV)

It's not what I see that requires faith, it's what I do not see.

Having the shield of faith made all the difference in my being successful in accomplishing the assignment that God had given me. Standing on God's promises was non-negotiable regardless of the status of my plight or the opinions of others regarding my plight. Faith in God must be a number one priority because without it, He cannot be pleased.

During the early stages of my assignment, in the spring of 1997, the enemy questioned my salvation and faith in numerous ways. His primary tactic involved a constant undermining of my service by comparing my actions or inactions with other church members' actions, suggesting that I possessed an inferior level of salvation or faith. And that comparison reflected the enemy's work in process!

The enemy also used my church attendance to create doubt within me. My wholehearted thought is that God's children should assemble because God's Word instructs them not to forsake gathering with other Christians. But the enemy used the times when I didn't attend church, when I missed a Sunday or two, to convict me of non-attendance by reiterating the lie that my salvation or faith lacked authenticity.

And then, of course, he planted negative seeds of thought at every opportunity regarding the fact that I worked longer hours than normal or when I spent precious time watching television or playing games, with the intent of knocking me off course.

> *Set your mind on things above, not on things on the earth.*
> Colossians 3:2 (NKJV)

These instructions re-centered and focused me on heavenly matters rather than on earthly distractions.

> *For the weapons of warfare are not carnal but mighty in God for pulling down strongholds, casting down arguments and every high thing that exalts itself against the knowledge of God, bringing every thought into captivity to the obedience of Christ...*
> 2 Corinthians 10:4-5 (NKJV)

In its simplest terms, the weapons of warfare are the same as the armor of God, truth, righteousness, the gospel of peace, faith, salvation, the word of God, and prayer.

Having access to this arsenal of weapons frightens the enemy because these weapons may be utilized as tools for resisting and standing against the enemy. The enemy's immediate goal has always been to attack and weaken my mind and then flood it with self-destructing schemes and maneuvers.

Many people have proclaimed that wasting a mind is a tragic loss or that an idle mind is the devil's workshop. But I found it profound when I heard Ron Carpenter preach a sermon called Mind World. In that sermon he stated that *what happens in your mind plays out in time.* His basic point illuminated the fact that the thoughts, convictions, and mental images that I held in my mind would eventually manifest in my external reality. What profundity!

This was a concept that captures the cause and effect of human behavior/thinking. And it is one that the enemy is accustomed to using, particularly since our minds are subjected time and time again to his trickery. This is why I deemed protecting my mind a priority for my successful and permanent vanquishing of the enemy. My mind had to be focused, watchful, and ready for action for whatever was thrown its way, or the devil would wreak all kinds of havoc in my life, in every way possible. And knowing his intentions, securing my faithfulness had to be my primary focus. So, I incorporated the words of Tony Evans, a renowned evangelical pastor, speaker, author, and widely syndicated radio and television broadcaster, who served as Senior Pastor of Oak Cliff Bible Fellowship, in Dallas, Texas, into my life. Pastor Evans's interpretation of faith is *faith is acting as if it is so, even when it's not so, so that it can be so, simply because God said so*. And in using that interpretation of faith, I found it easier to secure my faith.

The fifth aspect of the armor of God gave me the ability to speak the commands, promises, and protections of God with authority. As a teenager, God saw fit to equip me with the knowledge of Him and His word through studying and learning the Bible.

> *...and the sword of the Spirit, which is the word of God...*
> Ephesians 6:17 (NKJV)

During that time in my life, I didn't know that a weapon could be a reference to God's Word. Neither did it enter my mind that God's word could be used as a weapon. In fact, God's word being a weapon to be reckoned with was never on my radar. I may have read about it, but I didn't know what it meant or how to apply it. In reminiscing about my initial introduction, outside of Sunday School, to God's Word, the Bible Story series stored on my mother's family room bookshelf entered my mind. I recalled how God had piqued my interest and curiosity after reading the first book and how each book captivated me as I read the subsequent books.

The impact that the first book had on me astonished me. From carrying one book upstairs to my bedroom to carrying four at a time showed me that I was completely captivated with each successive book. The storyline mirrored the narratives of the Bible, beginning with the creation of heaven and earth and continuing through the history of mankind, covering key events like Noah's Ark, David and Goliath, the reign of King David, Solomon's wisdom, the birth and ministry of Jesus, and many other significant stories from the Bible. The series ended with the manifestation of God's original intent of living with and amid mankind. Reading these stories and a sense of being led by God's Spirit opened my mind and conditioned it to read many versions of the Bible including the King James Version, the New King James Version, the Amplified Version, the Message, among many others. God allocated every resource at his disposal for bestowing the knowledge, common sense, and prudence that I needed in deploying me for my assignment. I have also read commentaries that enhanced my cognizance with additional detailed explanations, interpretations, and analyses of scriptures, cultures, historical backgrounds, and biblical and theological significance. All of this supplemental material played a critical role in my learning and adopting a clearer interpretation of God's Word and the application of His word to my life. I saw the importance of daily reading, of memorizing and meditating on verses and passages that unveiled power and meaning to me, and of summoning God to direct His Word to become a living Word by Him planting it in my heart and in my mind.

I listened to local and national ministers, who used their gift of breaking God's Word down to bite-sized pieces and then serving it from perspectives that I never would have thought of.

Through the deep insight into God's Word that He has revealed and instilled in me, I know how to use Scripture to protect and uplift myself while also overcoming the enemy.

> *Out of the same mouth proceed blessing and cursing...*
> James 3:10 (NKJV)

This knowledge enables me to resist and cast out the evils that try to bind me through the power of speaking against them. God's Word is an excellent tool for striking the enemy, and it is the only tool that Satan respects and obey. It's the same tool that Jesus used when being tempted by the devil in Matthew 4:1-11.

Without God's Word, I would have been going to war with an enemy who had mastered using his weapons of war, which included throwing fiery darts, otherwise known as spiritual or psychological attacks, to destroy me without a weapon of my own. Under such circumstances, destruction and failure would have been inevitable. Because God is all-knowing, He ensured that I absorbed enough of His Word to initiate and pursue my assignment through early and continuous teachings of His Word and the experiences that I had over the course of my life.

The last piece of armor that I have listed above is praying and staying vigilant, which kept me connected to God, feeling confident, and possessing warm feelings of secure protection. But during the hardest and coldest moments, when I could not pray enough by myself, God had others praying with and for me. In fact, on some occasions the Spirt prayed for me because I didn't know what to pray.

> *Likewise, the Spirit also helps us in our weaknesses. For we do not know what we should pray for as we ought, but the Spirit Himself makes intercession for us with groanings which cannot be uttered.*
> Romans 8:26 (NKJV)

After gaining my full attention and focus, removing the spirit of fear, and equipping me with His armor, God advanced to the next critical step before being content with my readiness and ability to perform the assignment that He had predestined for me. And that step? Learning the enemy.

God introduced the enemy, Satan, to me through His Word and my own life experiences, as well as the experiences of others on a rather broad platform. In the early fall of 1997, I found a poem entitled *My Name is Cocaine* which described the personality of the enemy or devil that would be the enemy that bound Terry. Recently, I discovered the group Mînus released a song in 2003 with the same title and similar lyrics. I had never heard the personality of the enemy or devil depicted the way the poem captured it and with such accuracy. When researching the origin of the poem, at the time, Google found the author to be unknown and ChatGPT stated the poem was an anonymous piece so I'm unable to give the author the credit that he or she so richly deserves.

The clever, witty, and rhythmic way that the words flowed left me nodding in agreement and bent over in laughter at the same time. But as I digested every stanza and the meaning of each word resonated with the spirit in me, it helped me gain the ultimate realization of the nature of the evil that I would be tackling.

> *God is our refuge and strength, a very present help in trouble.*
> Psalms 46:1 (NKJV)

This is what finding this poem meant to me. It presented itself as help from God in grasping, interpreting, and combatting the evil that I would be facing. It targeted and landed dead-on in the center of the effect that crack cocaine had on its victims.

I was certain that this unknown author must have had some personal knowledge about crack cocaine addiction to have conveyed such an accurate description of the affects that crack cocaine has on people. The author accurately described feelings of pain, hurt, deceit, and devastation. The unknown author may not have known the impact that his or her description of crack cocaine would have on others, but I bet that the unknown author had no doubt as to the validity of his or her feelings.

As I read each word and related each sentence to my experience and interactions with friends and family who fell victim to crack cocaine, the author's words echoed through my entire being. The poem became a part of all of my future encounters, my story, and my life. For each sentence written, I could name someone, friend or acquaintance, who could testify to the truthfulness of the unknown author's words.

I didn't perceive the potency of the enemy I would face until I read this poem.

That at the name of Jesus every knee should bow, of those in heaven, and of those on earth, and of those under the earth, and that every tongue should confess that Jesus Christ is Lord, to the glory of God the Father.

Philippians 2:10-11 (NKJV)

This scripture gave me authority and dominion over the enemy. I knew that at the mention of Jesus' name, the enemy had to bow.

No weapon formed against you shall prosper, and every tongue which rises against you in judgment you shall condemn. This is the heritage of the servants of the Lord and their righteousness is from Me, says the Lord.

Isaiah 54:17 (NKJV)

And since God had removed the spirit of fear from me, placed His armor on me, and the identities of all persons who would have a role in the quest before me had been defined, everything had been set for me to move forward with my assignment. And with God on my side, who could be against me? For my victory had already been declared!

Victory is mine,

saith the Lord!

CHAPTER NINE

ON ASSIGNMENT

My husband, Terry, is the kindest, meekest, gentlest, loving, and thoughtful person I've ever met. His personality is genuine, and he has never met a stranger. He is the helping hand to all who encounter him, man, woman, child, and dog alike. He doesn't expect favors or rewards for his kindness. He does whatever he does out of the kindness of his heart. He's humbled, possesses an honest heart, and has a mind to serve the Lord. Terry works hard and takes pride in the work that he does.

In all of the years that I've known him, almost twenty-nine years and counting, I have never met a person who knows him, who has spoken an unkind word about his person or personality. He is incredible! From day one, he has shown me support, love, encouragement, and praise. He called me his Nubian Queen and nicknamed me Cuddles from the beginning of our relationship, and to this day he still calls me his Nubian Queen and Cuddles.

And the icing on the cake is that he has never treated my daughter as a stepdaughter. He treats her as if she is his own biological child. God could not have given me a better soulmate. Not long after meeting him, I wrote this poem to convey how I felt about him and our relationship:

New Love

Your touch so tender and so warm;
Such ecstasy I feel in your arms;
The realness of your words and heart;
My new love...my new start.

God gave me you when I was in need;
To have, to hold, someone to believe;
Someone I could love through thick and thin;
Someone whom I could befriend.

God has given me you, but God has also given you me;
To have, to hold, to be thought of as we;
Someone to love you, just for you;
Someone to share the things we both go through.

So, there's no doubt in what has been written;
Let it stay on your mind and never be hidden;
That the words of this poem are forever true;
Because God gave you me, and God has given me you.

I saw in Terry a meek heart, but so did Satan, the enemy of all mankind's soul, which is why early on in Terry's life Satan sought to destroy him. Though Terry and I did not know each other, or even live in the same city and state, during his high school years he experimented with alcohol and drugs, the same as I did, and for similar reasons. We wanted to fit in as we figured out our identities and who we thought we wanted to be while having what we called fun.

After high school, he worked at various places while continuing to use alcohol and drugs on a recreational basis, the same as I did and as many of our high school peers did. After all, hanging out with friends and enjoying two or three drinks while smoking a joint or two proved to be a pleasurable time, not a problem.

Terry married in his early twenties and had two children, Tera and Terrance. Based upon conversations that I have had with his ex-wife and children; I am convinced that he had genuine love and affection for his family and delivered provisions for them the best that he could. As time passed, however, the drug usage increased, which had a negative impact on his relationship, which then led to a divorce. This was not what he wanted, but he did not abandon his drug use. Feelings of hurt and disappointment overwhelmed him, and to feel better or to bury the pain he dove deeper into using drugs, changing the original purpose from having fun to escaping pain. And this change of purpose and motive, apparent or inapparent, shifted the course of his life.

This change had a long-term impact on his life, and it affected him and the people he loved. In fact, it confused the people who loved him most. His mom, his dad, his siblings, his children, and his close friends observed the downward spiral that became his life.

His identity altered, the things in which he took an interest slowly decreased, and the attributes in which he prided himself took a backseat to his increased desire to use drugs. Those who knew him well could not discern how this could have happened to him. His parents prayed without ceasing and solicited prayers from others, such as their pastor and family members and a trusted circle of friends. Yet, he stayed the course and fell deeper into drug use.

As his drug use impaired his ability to pursue and achieve his life's dreams, and as his resources dwindled, he turned to selling drugs to support a habit that had transformed from having fun into an addiction. For a while he maintained the status quo selling and using drugs, but over time the status quo led to an increased dependence on the drugs, despite continuous attempts to stop.

For more than twenty years, I witnessed Terry attempting to stop using drugs, but somehow, some way, he always ended up using again. And this pattern led him to jail numerous times. At some point, before meeting me, he admitted to himself that he had a problem and needed help, which led him to cry out to God.

On the day that I met Terry, November 18, 1996, he communicated to me that while in jail, he pleaded with God for help, and he knew that God sent him me. In hindsight, I too can agree that God sent me to help him navigate his way through obtaining additional knowledge regarding spiritual matters and having a sharper perception as to who God was, discovering God's Will for his life, and a permanent release of the dependence on drugs that plagued his life. Terry had trust in God, but his spiritual maturity was not developed enough to gain dominance over his addiction.

But God knew what He had instilled in me and knew that I could render the assistance, encouragement, comfort, and advocacy that Terry needed as God brought him to where He intended him to be.

> And the Lord God said, "It is not good that man should be alone; I will make him a helper comparable to him."
>
> Genesis 2:18 (NKJV)

God declared the same thing for Terry, so He sent me to be his helpmate. I welcomed it, but I didn't know what it entailed. It didn't take long for me to realize my role.

Sometime in the spring of 1997, Terry bought a 1983 Oldsmobile Toronado. Members of his immediate family shared positive opinions about the car, but a vague sense of skepticism—rooted in factors I couldn't quite identify—left me puzzled. I sensed that something unspoken, concealed beneath their apparent cynicism was at play. In fact, mumblings such as *See him when you see him* rolled from under the breath of some family members. Not knowing the meaning of these mumblings pushed me to make inquiries. Terry indicated that having a car would allow him to buy drugs without family members knowing his whereabouts. At times, he was gone for weeks at a time. I referred to the periods of time that he spent away as him being *off to the races* or *on one of his runs*.

A month after Terry purchased the Toronado, what that meant became evident to me. I hadn't heard from Terry for a month, and then he called from jail, saying that he had been arrested on a drug-related charge. For every day of that month, I prayed and proclaimed God's Word for him and on his behalf.

Terry being arrested and jailed permitted him to rest, the same way that a boxer rested in his corner after boxing a three-minute round. It gave him time to regroup. While in regrouping mode, he prayed, read God's Word, and did what he could to stay positive.

During this resting period, Terry quoted, "This is a small price to pay for a lifetime of happiness."

What he meant was that every experience of reprimand, discipline, consequence, and penalty led him closer to having a lifetime of freedom and happiness from drug addiction. He trusted that one day God would deliver him from his drug addiction, and he asserted that he would overcome his addiction. Though uncertain of the exact date and time of the end of his addiction, he presumed that in God's time, it would happen.

Terry was released from jail after three months of incarceration. He landed a job the day after his release. He worked for two weeks, received his paycheck, and in a day or two, he found himself broke again. In one of our conversations, I probed for answers as to how he spent his entire paycheck within a day or two.

"Terry, you can't be spending all of your money on drugs. Otherwise, you would have been hospitalized for an overdose."

"I don't spend all my money on drugs. Sometimes I pay for a place to use the drugs. I also buy beer or alcohol, cigarettes, and food for myself and others."

"Why? That's crazy. I've never heard of such nonsense! Why don't you bring the drugs to my house, use them in the bathroom, and save some damn money?"

He tried that once or twice, but I think that he either preferred using with others, or he didn't want me to see him while he was using drugs or after. During this time, I smoked cigarettes and perhaps a joint from time to time. My weed-smoking days had decreased from my days of living in New Orleans in the 1980s, before moving to San Jose, but every now and then I could be tempted to take a pull or two off a joint.

Sometimes while Terry was on one of his runs, I visited his mother's house, where he stayed, during my lunch break or after work, and shook holy anointing oil all over his room. I prayed in his room and proclaimed God's Word over his life. At times, we even prayed together.

After being sober for a month or two and after being released from jail, Terry's addiction sent him to the races anew. A month later, he called and announced that he had been arrested again. One or two months later, another arrest. Since his first arrest, God had blessed me with access to an excellent attorney through one of my co-workers, Catherine. Upon learning that Terry had been arrested, she introduced me to Kyle Collins, and he became Terry's attorney.

Kyle had great success representing Terry. The first time that Terry used Kyle's services, he had to pay fees and fines, but he avoided incarceration. Terry repeated his disappearing and being arrested act. By his third arrest, the judge imposed other stipulations in lieu of incarceration, which included fees, fines, and completion of the Travis County one-year Short Program beginning March 18, 1998. This program is now known as the Smart Program.

The Short Program was an outpatient program that proved beneficial for Terry. The program concentrated on stabilization, self-improvement, and transition into the community by addressing the mental, emotional, and educational needs of an individual. At the completion of the program, the arrest and conviction that had led him to the Short Program would be expunged from his criminal record.

In March of 1999, Terry completed the Short Program as planned, resulting in the expungement of his arrest and conviction from his criminal record. Throughout the entire program I prayed alone, as well as with friends and family. I meditated on God's Word and stood in confidence that God would break through the stronghold of Terry's addiction because I knew within my spirit that God delivers those He loves from addictions and other sorts of bad habits.

After Terry's release from the Short Program, God spoke to my spirit and indicated that He wanted me to move Terry out of the environment that appeared to hinder his progress, so I encouraged him to live with me in the suburbs of Austin. Internally, I had an issue with this because I didn't feel that God wanted us to be shacking up or living together without being married. Before speaking to Terry about him moving in with me, I prayed about my decision for a week, and God placed in my heart that He didn't have a problem with us sleeping under the same roof.

However, He did have a problem with us having sex. He expected us not to sleep together. But because He needed Terry away from familiar areas infested with drugs or environments that could remind or entice him to use them, God trusted me to do my best to follow what I knew he wanted me to do. He relied on me to be strong. Although we did not have sex often, I found myself in a perpetual state of repentance until we married. By that point, repentance had become a habit.

Being away from the areas where Terry typically purchased drugs helped, but it didn't eliminate the problem. Whenever Terry had transportation, he remained in the race. With every hint of progress, the enemy pressed harder. With rigorous prayers, I sought additional information on spiritual warfare, leading me to fast for three or four days at a time. The Bible teaches one to fast when loosening bonds of wickedness and breaking yokes (strongholds).

> *Is this not the fast that I have chosen: To loosen the bonds of wickedness, to undo the heavy burdens, to let the oppressed go free, and that you break every yoke?*
>
> Isaiah 58:8 (NKJV)

> *And when he had come into the house, His disciples asked Him privately, "Why could we not cast it out?" So, He said to them, "This kind can come out by nothing but prayer and fasting."*
>
> Mark 9:28-29 (NKJV)

The Making of a Warrior: A Tool for Living A Victorious Life workbook furnished me with advanced knowledge of spiritual warfare. It helped me with being a worshipping warrior, which is defined in the workbook as winners (believers in Jesus Christ) who combat and prevail against the forces of hell through a dynamic lifestyle of magnifying God.

> *For you died, and your life is hidden with Christ in God.*
> Colossians 3:3 (NKJV)

As a worshipping warrior, I could identify the attacks of the enemy, and I was able to discern further God's way of accomplishing what He had already predestined for me to accomplish.

Due to my familiarity with the roles that God, Jesus, and the Holy Spirit played in my life, recognizing the schemes, plans, methods, plots, and stratagems, better referred to in the workbook, as the wiles of the devil (the enemy) evolved into my primary focus, along with gaining insight into how his kingdom operated. The workbook teaches that God has a kingdom, as does the devil. The definition of Kingdom is a form of government in which a king or queen serves as a supreme ruler. In God's Kingdom, God is the supreme ruler, and in the devil's kingdom, the devil (Satan) is the supreme ruler.

As I dove into the workbook, I felt myself re-fueling, transforming into a stronger more knowledgeable, focused, and powerful person. God knew what I needed to move forward with the assignment that he had given me.

My spirit felt on fire! It felt elated and ready to take on the assignment of helping my husband overcome his drug addiction. I was ready to go the extra mile, wherever that mile would lead me.

I prayed without ceasing.

> *Epaphras.... always laboring fervently for you in prayers, that you may stand perfect and complete in all the will of God.*
> Colossians 4:12 (NKJV)

It felt like laboring because I put in great effort to pray, praying even while engaged in other activities. While I worked at my place of employment, I found myself praying as I completed tasks and projects. One time

I received an award for a project that I completed, and I didn't even realize that I had performed the work. I must have done it subconsciously.

After learning about the many wiles of the devil, the hierarchy of his kingdom, and how it operated, I proceeded forward with a deeper commitment to helping Terry. Examples of this included me locating him during those times when he went off to the races. At least five or six times my mother-in-law called me to inform me that Terry hadn't returned to her house when she expected him to. After calling him, and after his voicemail picked up time after time, I knew that this was just another day at the races for him.

The first time that I received a phone call from my mother-in-law, my initial reaction led me to pray for direction from God. "Lord, what is it that you want me to do?"

I heard in my heart, *Drive your car to Riverside Drive, and I will direct you from there.* Once on Riverside Drive, I heard the Lord speak to my heart again. *Continue forward, turn left at the light, then look to your left, and you will see him at the Exxon.*

And, lo and beyond, there he stood next to his car. Though I knew that God could do anything, my amazement overwhelmed me. God using me to locate Terry at numerous places, such as hotels, apartments, run-down neighborhoods, and clubs flabbergasted me because of my limited familiarity with the streets of Austin. I spent my working hours in central Austin and my evening hours in northwest Austin, which is twenty to thirty minutes away from central Austin.

Outside of work and visiting Terry's parent's house, I didn't have a reason to be in central Austin, so I didn't learn many places in central Austin. Northwest Austin offered all forms of shopping and entertainment, which meant that I didn't have a need to patronize the businesses in central Austin. My limited familiarity with central Austin made locating Terry, with God's help, even more astonishing, and this increased my confidence and faith in God's abilities and power.

When looking for Terry, I found myself in crack-infested neighborhoods, where I usually found him or other evidence of his having been there, such as his car or someone who knew him. Sometimes God led me to pray out loud, asking him to rebuke the evil forces that had infiltrated a particular middle- to upper-middle-class neighborhood and destroyed the original beauty of it. On three or four occasions God instructed me to bring anointing oil, also referred to as holy oil. The practice of anointing people and places with holy oil holds significant meaning in the Bible and in Christian tradition. The act of anointing with holy oil serves as a powerful symbol of consecration, healing, and divine empowerment.

Upon entering a drug infested neighborhood, God inspired me to pull over and throw a splash of holy oil in the air before praying that He would uproot the evil that had taken over the neighborhood. The use of holy oil had been a common practice for me because the churches that I attended taught and practiced it.

> *Then you shall take the anointing oil and anoint the tabernacle and all that is in it and consecrate it and all its furnishings; and it shall be holy.*
>
> Exodus 30:26 (NIV)

> *And they cast out many demons, and anointed with oil many who were sick, and healed them.*
>
> Mark 6:13 (NKJV)

I'm not certain of the precise moment or day that God began or finished uprooting the evil that had taken over the neighborhoods He had me anoint with oil, but ten to fifteen years later, when visiting those same areas, I was filled with awe as I gazed upon the results of God driving out the evil that plagued those neighborhoods. I noted with joy the new structures and landscapes surrounded by immaculate, fresh chic décor that replaced the dilapidated buildings and homes destroyed by drug infestation. Newcomers to the central Austin area would never know that those places once harbored drug addicts and all sorts of other drug-related activities.

On another occasion during my quest to find Terry, I saw his Toronado being driven around by a young boy. Whenever Terry ended up in jail, he always managed to retrieve his car from the impound lot, or he arranged for me or a relative to take it to a safe place while he was in jail. This time Terry had been out of jail for a month, maybe two months, before running off to the races again. The boy driving his car looked like he couldn't have been older than 19 or so. I did a U-turn and sped up to follow the boy, thinking that he would lead me to Terry. But instead of leading me to Terry, he led me away from him to a house where he, a lady, and a baby either lived or planned to visit.

As he exited the Toronado, I rushed up to him and demanded that he give me my car. Though the car belonged to Terry, I wanted the young boy to think that the car belonged to me, so I called it my car. He wouldn't know the precise owner of the car.

The boy explained, "Ma'am, I rented this car from Terry. I thought that the car belonged to him."

I snapped back, "No, this is my car, and I want it back! If you don't give it back to me, I will call the police and have you arrested for stealing my car."

The young boy looked afraid, so I gave him another option. "If you would like, you can take me to whoever gave you my car, otherwise, I'm calling the police."

"Ma'am, I'll take you to him. Just let me tell my girl that I'm leaving."

Though the boy didn't know it, and I may have appeared to be brave and fearless, my heart nearly leapt out of my chest with apprehension. But during this interaction, I felt like the queen of the jungle.

The young boy returned to Terry's car, though he thought that it belonged to me, and drove me straight to where Terry was. When I pulled up behind the boy and Terry saw me, the look on his face was priceless. Utter confusion. I know that he had to think, *What the heck is going on.*

"Thank you." I extended my hand toward the boy to retrieve the car key.

I don't recall the young boy and Terry even acknowledging one another. I walked up to Terry and ordered him to drive the car home.

He didn't say anything. He humbly followed my order. Looking back, I suspect the young boy lived in the area where he led me to Terry. At the time, it never occurred to me how he made his way back home—or how he returned to the young woman and baby he had dropped off at the spot where I first began following him to Terry.

After entering my apartment, I headed straight for my holy oil and approached Terry with it. I opened the bottle and sent a generous sprinkle his way. With direct eye contact, I spoke beyond the conscious Terry to his spirit. I informed Terry that the person to whom I was speaking was not him, rather it was Satan.

I pointed my finger at Terry's eyes. "Satan, I see you in there. You must leave now!"

To ensure that Satan had a way out, I opened the front door and commanded him to depart from Terry and go to the abyss. In the Bible, the abyss is often a term used to denote a deep, unfathomable place, typically associated with chaos, darkness, or a place of imprisonment or punishment.

> And they begged Him that He would not command them to go out
> into the abyss.
>
> Luke 8:31 (NKJV)

That night, Terry showered and rested. I wish that I could say that because Satan had been called out of him, Terry's drug addiction ended. It didn't. In fact, it got worst, and I'm thinking that that was because Terry let Satan back in.

> When an unclean spirit goes out of a man, he goes through dry
> places, seeking rest, and finds none... Then he goes and takes with
> him seven other spirits more wicked than himself, and they enter
> and dwell there; and the last state of that man is worse than the
> first...
>
> Matthew 12:43, 45 (NKJV)

Two weeks later, Terry ran off to the races again. Though God had previously given me geographical instructions in locating Terry, this time, God had directed me not to go looking for him. God had placed in my heart that His purpose in sending me to find Terry had been accomplished. My running him down in a city in which my familiarity with that city limited my chances of finding him led Terry to see that he could not hide from God because God knew his every move. There's no way that I would have known the places where I found him on my own.

Because this baffled Terry and made him wonder how I knew his whereabouts, he figured that the only explanation had to be God. And that was the conclusion God wanted Terry to reach—that he couldn't hide, that he couldn't hide because God was always with him. And with that, God sending me to smoke Terry out of his hiding places ended.

My initial response to his disappearance after God indicated He didn't want me to search for him any longer, was to search for him on my own, but I could not find him. I heard God whisper to me; *I told you that I didn't need you to locate him anymore.* And from that point, I ceased all efforts toward finding him. For some reason, this didn't bother me. In fact, I felt rather relieved, but I could hear in my mother-in-law's voice that my not trying any further to corral Terry disappointed her. I think that she felt disappointed because her sense of relief and assurance that I would find him and bring him to safety was no longer there. This made my heart go out for her, which is why her harboring any ill feelings towards me never concerned me, though I could relate to the anxiety that she may have felt thinking of the dangers in which Terry may have placed himself. However, our prayers and trust in God gave her a modicum of comfort and peace.

Terry disappeared even more, and, as in the past, he didn't stop until he got arrested. This time the judge sentenced him to three months in jail. With three months in jail and no funds to pay his car note, the bank repossessed his car. Because he was not responsible in owning a car and because having a car afforded him too much opportunity, access, and freedom, which all played a major role in preventing him from controlling his drug urges, I applauded the repossession of his car and didn't look forward to him replacing it anytime soon.

In the spring of 2000, Terry's release from jail enabled him to work two jobs, both near our home. Since Terry's Toronado had been repossessed, Terry rode the bus to both jobs. And when I could, I picked him up. Throughout the entire time I've known Terry, God has always blessed him with the ability to land a job. I think it's Terry's personality, attitude, and God's power to touch the hearts of hiring managers that pushes hiring managers to open the door and give a second, third, and fourth chance to a convicted drug offender such as Terry.

At one of his jobs, Terry had access to the company's van for transporting clients to and from appointments and other types of outings. With this access, it didn't take long for temptation to creep in, causing another episode of Terry being off to the races, and like the other times, it didn't end until his arrest. In July 2000, Terry received an Unauthorized Use of a Motor Vehicle charge. This time the judge set bail at two hundred dollars. I retrieved his check from his employer and paid the bail. Two days later, Terry was arrested anew for possession of a synthetic drug, which is a drug that was considered to be fake crack.

Terry faced two charges, for which he could have been sentenced to five, if not more, years in prison. I was ambivalent about the prospect of him spending so many years in prison. I felt a sense of relief because with him locked up, at least I would know where he was. But I hated the thought of not being with him. Outside of his drug addict behavior, nothing about him belonged behind bars.

My heart and my mind ached, and this could not have been a more stressed time for me because the enemy never ceased attacking my faith with negative thoughts. Every time that Terry ran off to the races, the enemy threw fiery darts of doubt at me. *God's not going to deliver him. You see what he's doing, and it's going to always be this way because he's a loser. And it doesn't matter what God has shown you, he's never going to amount to anything, he's worthless. Once a loser, always a loser.*

The enemy threw a different flaming missile to attack my confidence and replace it with insecurity. *He's going to die out there running after that dope. He's not thinking about you. You think you, alone, are his woman. When he's not in your bed, he's in another woman's bed, and he's calling her bed home.*

But God reminded me that the enemy is a liar and the father of lies.

> *...for he is a liar and the father of it.*   John 8:44 (NKJV)

The enemy is in opposition to God's wants and desires for His children's lives. And whenever God speaks, so be it because He is God, and it is impossible for Him to lie. And as for what I saw happening with my own eyes, He comforted my spirit with His gentle voice when he whispered to me, *You must walk by faith and not by sight.*

While Terry awaited his sentencing, I stayed in constant prayer and supplication for his deliverance from his drug addiction. One evening, while in fervent prayer, I felt a snapping in my stomach.

I whispered to God, "Lord, what was that?"

I heard His soft, still voice. *It is done. The yoke has been broken.* In the Bible, this phrase symbolizes freedom from oppression, bondage, or a burden. So, in essence, God had informed me that Terry's bondage to drugs had been broken from a spiritual perspective. The physical deliverance, Terry no longer using drugs, remained to be seen, but through faith it would be realized with continued praise and dependency on God.

Upon receiving this message from God, I praised and worshipped Him to the point where my flesh surrendered, and my spirit took control. How sensational my spirit felt! I felt like that moment could not be interrupted or interfered with because in that moment, I resided in a different place and time.

While being engulfed in the effects of the spirit, I received a phone call from my father-in-law. In a state of euphoric, I blurted out what I had just experienced moments before answering his call.

Unmoved by my euphoric state, he proceeded with his agenda. "Vivian, why did you tell Terry that I would not help him get out of jail?"

"Because that's what you told me to tell him when I called you with the news that he had been arrested."

"Yeah, I know, but I didn't mean that."

"Well, I didn't know that you didn't mean that."

"You shouldn't have relayed that to him."

"I'm sorry. I thought that that's what you wanted me to convey to him."

"Well, no, I didn't. Okay, bye." He hung up the phone.

My heart sank into the pit of my stomach. I felt so hurt and disappointed. I had transmitted the message exactly as it had been given to me. But more important than that, I felt that the fact that the yoke had been broken should have taken precedence and caused instant celebration and rejoicing. And when it did not, I felt stripped of my joy.

God knew my heart and in the snap of a finger replaced those disheartened feelings with forgiveness because I knew deep within my heart the amount of unwavering love that Terry's dad had for his son. And his calling when he did was designed by the enemy to interfere with my praise and worship and the goodness with which I felt God was showering me. I loved my father-in-law, and I knew that his heart would always beat for his son's deliverance. So, him not responding in the manner in which I thought he should have responded, at that moment, was of no consequence to me.

I had waited from 1997 to the end of 1999 for a breakthrough, and now that I had gotten some indication that a breakthrough had occurred, praising and exalting God, right then, jumped to the top of my list of priorities. I praised God until I fell asleep.

The next morning, *It is done. The yoke has been broken.* played over and over in my mind.

I recall thinking to myself, *What does that mean.* Those kinds of thought-provoking questions have always led me to call my spiritual advisor, Stacey, to seek her opinion. Together, we searched the scriptures.

...That I will break his yoke from your neck and will burst your bonds...

Jeremiah 30:8 (NKJV)

I will go before you and make the crooked places straight; I will break in pieces the gates of bronze and cut the bars of iron.

Isaiah 45:2 (NKJV)

The Lord your God, who goes before you, He will fight for you, according to all He did for you in Egypt before your eyes.

Deuteronomy 1:30 (NKJV)

The revelation that we gained from these scriptures taught us that God's Spirit works on our behalf and that what He does in the Spirit may occur prior to its physical manifestation. What this meant for Terry is that the yoke had been broken from a spiritual perspective, but the physical manifestation lay somewhere in the future. I had no idea when, what, or how the physical manifestation would be ushered in, however, I felt confident that, someday, it would be.

Although Terry faced two charges, by the time he received a sentence of five months at a correctional center due to the possession of a synthetic drug charge being dropped, he had already served three months out of the five because his case kept getting postponed and then reset. Upon his release from the correctional center in September 2000, the judge ordered him to check himself into the Salvation Army Rehab to complete their three-month rehabilitation program.

By this point, I felt worn down, exasperated, and exhausted. It seemed like I couldn't discern in which direction I needed to go, forward or backwards. I even declared that I would leave him and walk away from the entire situation. I felt that I had reached my breaking point. In those moments, God interrupted those thoughts and replaced them with memories of my own battle with cigarette addiction and my many failings, how often I promised to quit smoking cigarettes and/or marijuana, fornicating, stealing cigarettes or office supplies, and other petty crimes. Despite knowing better, I persisted, and God continued to forgive me. These reflections realigned my thoughts and kept me committed to my assignment.

The Salvation Army rehab program approved Terry to participate in off-campus outings, such as visits to my house, picnics in the park, horseback riding, and whatever fun we wanted to have if he returned before his 8:00 p.m. curfew. The support that I gave to Terry through my faithfulness, loyalty, and commitment to him led him to question the origin of my love, despite him considering me to be a dedicated supporter of him through his drug addiction recovery.

One day he inquired, "Where on earth does your love come from?"

"Not from on earth, that's for sure. It comes from God. It's called unconditional love."

Though Terry remained silent, I heard God's voice in my spirit whisper, *Exactly!* Like a lightbulb moment, I felt like God high-fived Jesus *She has it!* He revealed to me that day that my role involved showing and practicing His unconditional love. That's the assignment that I had been chosen to perform in a nutshell. No matter what, my greatest and chief weapon in achieving success in my assignment was something that I possessed within myself, God's unconditional love. This meant that I was to show Terry love regardless of his shortcomings, faults, and successes by offering him advice, ideas, and a shoulder to cry on whenever he needed one and without brutal judgement. Including me in his support system gave him the help that he needed from a person without a real dog in the fight. Terry's drug addiction was his, not mines, but God placed me there to help him.

God had established, before introducing me to Terry, my total independence, and my dependence upon Him and Him alone. I could pay my own rent, my own car note, purchase food and other necessities, and take full responsibility for my daughter without the assistance of another person. Having this level of independence affirmed that I could show Terry pure, unadulterated love without any other complicating factors. So, when Terry saw or felt the love that I had to offer, he would know that that love had no conditions and that it originated with God.

How awesome is the wisdom of God! I did not know Terry's mind, but God did. He knew Terry's exact need, love with no expectations. Most people expect their family members to love them, but a stranger loving them isn't a typical expectation.

God sent me to Terry as a stranger, free of any hidden expectations or conditions, knowing that I would be the clearest lens through which Terry could witness His love.

> *For God so loved the world that He gave His only begotten Son...*
> John 3:16 (NKJV)

And God continues to give and show His love to all of mankind. What a mighty and loving God!

Terry completed his program with the Salvation Army by Christmas of 2000. I continued to offer my support. As a supporter, as described above, of a person on a odyssey through drug addiction, the probability of me stopping Terry from using drugs was slim to none and completely outside of my control. However, exercising God's unconditional love *was* within my control.

I have spoken to at least a dozen drug users over the last ten to fifteen years, and the one common theme among them all is the continuous love that their supporters showed them by not giving up on them. Terry put forth great effort to stay sober and successfully did so most of the time. Though I felt proud of his success, I knew that living life without his own transportation could not be the solution and that one day he would purchase a new car. And that, I must admit, I dreaded, yet I confidently declared that I would stand by him even then.

Affording continuous love to someone is much easier to talk about than to actually do because the enemy tries day and night to prevent drug addicts from feeling loved because when there is an absence of love, hopelessness thrives and, in many cases, recovery is lost. All of the biblical knowledge and weapons of war that I've learned about in preparing me for this assignment played a defining role in keeping me in a position to show love.

From the end of 2000 to May of 2001, the enemy threw additional fiery darts as I continued affirming my love, proclaiming God's Word, praising and worshipping God, and laboring in prayer, despite the hurt and pain that I endured with every episode of Terry using drugs. It felt like an ongoing battle or fight between me and the enemy, an imaginary battlefield that kept us both engaged.

The disappointment of Terry succumbing to his drug urges crushed my heart to the point of despair. The one victory that I felt that God had given me, other than Terry's life, is that the length of time that he spent at the races shortened significantly. Instead of being gone for weeks at a time, his disappearances decreased to a few days at a time, and because he didn't have transportation, he also didn't get arrested.

Though God had given me a few friends and relatives to console me, for the most part, I felt alone. I didn't want to involve my mother, my father, or my sisters because while it might have been easy for me to forgive Terry for the obstacles that we faced and endured, I didn't want to put my family members in a position of having to forgive him. For what they did know about Terry's situation, they accepted him with open arms, encouraged him, and showed him unconditional love as well. And I am so thankful and beholden to my family for that.

I recall one time, during one of my loneliest moments, I wrote a letter to the Lord entitled, *Lord, I Cry from the Battlefield.*

> *Once again, I showed up on the battlefield, and my troop is me and You. The rest are spectators with words that are heard across the field, but for real, where's the sword, the breastplate, the help that can take away some of the fear and loneliness? For the rest is a struggle between the wills, the will to let go and the will to hold on, but the feelings are strong, and the wrestling within is steep and deep within my soul. My spirit is so willing, and my flesh is willing yet so weak so that it's killing and healing as one,*

and in time, it will rule and make bold statements of my
prevailing as history unfolds the inevitable.

    On this field alone with no other, I suffer in silence this
unbearable battle and struggle, that leads to victory as my
cry from the battlefield takes its place in history. Yes! A win
for our troop — me and You.

Feelings of distress threatened to drown me, and thoughts that I should cut my losses and move on were louder than my heartbeat, which was yelling at me to hang in there. God had spoken to me about my assignment, so when my minister, a close friend or two, and co-workers who knew my situation indicated that God would not direct me to have a relationship with a person with a drug addiction and that perhaps co-dependency had set in and I needed to seek help for myself, I wondered if they were correct.

> *...the Lord said to Hosea: Go, take yourself a wife of harlotry and*
> *children of harlotry for the land has committed great harlotry by*
> *departing from the Lord.*
>
> Hosea 1:2 (NKJV)

In other words, God had instructed Hosea to marry a prostitute, someone who would not, perhaps even could not, be loyal to him. How much different is that from a drug addict and his ability to be loyal to his relationships?

What I have learned and live by is that God leads us to where He needs us, which will be a place for which He has already equipped us to occupy. God's children cannot be dismayed because being equipped doesn't mean that the task at hand won't be difficult. My entire life had consisted of me being trained and conditioned for the assignment that He had given me. I discovered this in hindsight, because while walking within my assignment, it felt like I had been thrown into the deep end of a pool and that I had to tread water just to survive.

In October 2000, the City of Austin's Aviation Department hired me as their Human Resources Advisor. Though Terry had a criminal record, a contracting company for the Airport Hilton Hotel hired him as a full-time driver couple of months after I started my job with the Aviation Department. People with criminal records can be hired to work at the airport in areas that do not require the employee to access the airport's secured areas. Since his company required him to be only in strictly non-secured areas of the airport, his criminal history didn't present a problem for him. Terry worked at night, and I worked during the day. We lived twenty miles away from the airport. I dropped him off at night, picked him up in the morning, took him home, and then proceeded to my job.

After seven months of putting eighty miles a day on my car, in May of 2001, we moved to an apartment in Del Valle, Texas, which was across the street from the Austin Bergstrom International Airport located in Austin, Texas. A tremendous savings in gas and wear and tear on my vehicle resulted from our move. Though Terry's drug use had improved quite a bit, the enemy continued to attack my faith by distracting Terry from time to time causing him to stray and chase drugs. The major difference between then and in the past was the length of time for which he strayed. For the most part, it occurred on his days off. He pulled himself together enough to work on the days that he was scheduled to work.

In our new apartment, one of his drug episodes led to an arrest. This time he did two months at the local jail, which was located a mile or two from our apartment. The irony of passing our apartment, when returning from court appearances or jail, was more than an irony. Once released, he secured another night job at the airport. This time he worked for the Parking Spot, formerly Parking Express, which is a local shuttle company that services the airport. As I stated before, God always blessed him with work. And He always blessed me with financial increases to my salary.

Give, and it will be given to you: good measure, pressed down,
shaken together, and running over will be put into your bosom.
For with the same measure that you use, it will be measured back
to you.

Luke 6:38 (NKJV)

I'm convinced that God blessed me whenever I practiced obedience to His Will as it pertained to my support of and my relationship with Terry. I could see God strengthening both Terry and me, but I didn't see the next step that He had planned for our lives, our marriage.

In July of 2002, Terry asked me to marry him. I didn't see us getting married anytime soon because our primary focus had been on him recovering from his drug addiction. I thought perhaps someday we would get married; however, Terry had indicated that he didn't see himself getting married again. But that didn't deter me from wanting to marry him one day because he had no idea what the future would hold so he couldn't predict whether we would end up married or not. But, at the time, his addiction prevented me from thinking along those lines.

In response to his proposal, I accepted, but I prayed to God to show me His Will regarding my marrying Terry. After meditating and waiting on His answer for two or three days, God placed on my heart that I should indeed marry Terry. He instructed me to plan the wedding, and He would ensure that the money necessary would be there.

We set the date of our wedding for November 23, 2002. And, as God had promised, the money and/or the services that we needed poured in. The wedding that we planned would have cost $8,000.00 to $9,000.00, but because God led our family and friends to offer their services and gifts, we ended up paying, out of pocket, $2,000.00 to $3,000.00, which came from our collective paychecks. Three weeks after Terry's proposal, the realtor I had been working with for two or three years in my efforts to purchase real estate called regarding a house for sale. I had been trying to buy a house, but my credit wouldn't qualify me for one.

I hadn't been able to list Terry on the lease of the new apartment because of his criminal history, so I indicated to the apartment manager that Erika and I would be living there for a short while and that, from time to time, my boyfriend would visit because I intended to build a house. Well, magically, rather than manufacturing the truth, I predicted the future.

God prevailed over the requirements for financing a house and gave us favor by permitting our approval for financing to purchase a house in Del Valle, Texas, approximately ten minutes from Austin and our jobs. We purchased an inventory home from KB Home, and we were also approved by KB Home to make minor changes to the original specs. I guess that I exercised my faith in purchasing a house by speaking to the apartment complex manager what did not exist as if it did exist.

> *...God, who gives life to the dead and calls those things which do not exist as though they did;*
>
> Romans 4:17 (NKJV)

We closed on our first home on November 22, 2002, we got married on November 23, 2002, and we moved into our new house on December 1, 2002. Also in December of 2002, Terry left the Parking Spot and began employment with another shuttle company located at the airport called Fast Park.

CHAPTER TEN

THE AFTERMATH — STANDING YOUR GROUND

So, God had done it. The yoke had been broken, we had been united in matrimony, we lived in our brand-new house, and Terry worked for a new shuttle company. On the surface, our lives appeared to be going well. Terry had almost quit using crack, his drug of choice, however, he substituted drinking beer and wine, and smoking weed to feed his addiction.

The enemy had convinced Terry that he didn't have a problem with drinking and smoking weed because this didn't include his drug of choice. The enemy had tricked him into thinking that he could quit drinking and smoking anytime he chose.

We had entered the aftermath, the period of time when extreme caution was necessary because Terry had moved beyond the stage of being an active crack user. As he began to accept the possibility of a life free from crack—though not yet from addiction itself—visible changes took hold in his body, mind, and soul: he had more energy, renewed motivation and clarity for future planning, and a restored sense of hope and purpose. While he wasn't entirely free of addiction, he was undeniably one step closer to true freedom than he had been before.

This critical time forced the enemy to use an arsenal of wiles for distracting and creating obstacles to interfere with the progress already made. He bombarded Terry with physical ailments that limited his participation in the physical activities he had once enjoyed, such as playing basketball and jogging. He often felt concerned about the effects that the drugs may have had on his organs and mental capacity. By attacking him in this way, slipping into a pity party or feelings of helplessness were inevitable. Thinking of what he used to do or used to be able to do depressed him and caused anxiety for him. The enemy often tormented him with such debilitating thoughts and doubts, yet, even to my surprise, he didn't allow it to break him.

Preoccupation with relationships that were either lost or damaged due to addiction presented itself as a danger as well because this resulted in him feeling guilt and shame. This almost always led to an excuse to relapse and to suppress the hurt and pain from past actions that had caused the loss or damage of the relationship. Thoughts of squandered possibilities flooded his mind, which included regrets over lost jobs or potential jobs. Quite often he thought about if he had not had his addiction; he would have been much further along with his life accomplishments. He thought about how his criminal record prevented him from obtaining positions that could have led to a lucrative career for him. I used to call it the woulda-shoulda-coulda syndrome.

Thinking too much about the many achievements that he would/should/could have earned sometimes overwhelmed him, which then caused further depression, hurt, and pain. So, falling too deep into these types of thoughts could be a definite trigger for relapsing. He had made it through his worst days, but the end still seemed so far away.

But to triumph during the aftermath, standing on faith remained key. I cannot emphasize that enough. Every area of weakness and spiritual growth had been unmasked and was subject to attack. Even the known truths, truths that he had always known to be true, appeared to be untrue. For instance, him knowing that he could not sustain himself, sometimes it appeared as if he could, placing him at risk for relapse due to failure to rely on God rather than himself.

My grace is sufficient for you, for My strength is made perfect in weakness.

II Corinthians 12:9 (NKJV)

This scripture assured him that relying on Christ should always be the option because whenever weakness kicks in, God's strength could and would sustain him.

During the aftermath, the enemy knew that his defeat had been pronounced by God because from a spiritual perspective, he, too, knew that God had broken the yoke. This period caused desperation for the enemy and demanded that he try his hardest to snag Terry and recapture his hold on him. The enemy is a sore loser, not a quitter. But God and I are not quitters, either!

The Bible teaches that Satan is the father of lies. And I've witnessed him throwing every lie both imaginable and unimaginable at me and everyone around me. The enemy's entire mission is to cause doubt in what God spoke or promised. But through pure faith both Terry and I were certain that he would be victorious over the enemy's arsenal of wiles.

God placed on my heart that no matter what or how the circumstances appeared, I should always speak, trust, and claim His promises.

Let him ask in faith, with no doubting, for he who doubts is like a wave of the sea driven and tossed by the wind. For let not that man suppose that he will receive anything from the Lord; he is a double-minded man, unstable in all his ways.

James 1:6-8 (NKJV)

The best analogy that I can think of that describes the aftermath are the tremors that results after a massive earthquake. The major damage is caused by the actual earthquake, but the tremors linger and can cause some damage as the earth settles. This is the same with drug addiction. The major damage for Terry occurred during the periods when he went off to the races, drugging non-stop until he ended up in jail. During the aftermath, the drug use didn't cause much damage. He might have left for a day, maybe even two if it was the weekend. This weighed on my heart like a game of tug-of-war, but I was comforted a bit by knowing that he would not be gone like he used to be.

From December of 2002 until March of 2003, I saw tremendous growth in Terry's prayer life. He sought God's Word more, which played a huge part in him lowering his guard and being more susceptible to God's Will and the direction in which God wanted to lead him.

Terry reminded me of a baby learning to walk. He took one step and fell, crawled to a table to lift himself up, and then took one or two more steps, and fell again. This cycle repeated itself, but between falls, I could see his strength building. And watching this pattern of behavior helped strengthen my faith and kept me from wavering. Giving up on my faith or on Terry could not and would not be an option for me.

I had no idea how long the aftermath would last. In the story of the Israelites in the Bible, in the books of Exodus, Leviticus, Numbers, Deuteronomy, and Joshua, after the Israelites were released from captivity in Egypt and crossed the Red Sea, they wandered in the wilderness for forty years before they took possession of the land that God had promised Abraham, their forefather, referred to as the Land of Milk and Honey. I consider these forty years to be the aftermath because the Israelites had been set free from captivity (the yoke broken) but had not yet taken possession of the Land of Milk and Honey (the physical manifestation of the promise). And during that forty-year span, God used that opportunity to develop, mature, and position the Israelites and their descendants to enter the promised land. I hoped with every fiber of my being that it wouldn't take that long for the physical manifestation of Terry's complete deliverance from drug addiction to materialize.

In 2003, God led both Terry and me to join a church in which we could both grow. We visited two or three churches before joining Greater Mount Zion Baptist Church (GMZ) under the leadership of Pastor Gaylon Clark.

While enjoying the services, I stood next to Terry as Pastor Clark opened the doors of discipleship and requested that all who wanted to be saved or who needed a church home (to become a member of his church community) to proceed to the alter. I had hoped that Terry wanted to join, but I didn't want to suggest it or influence his decision to join, so I stood in silence as Terry indicated that we should join the pastor at the alter. Terry had been a member of the church his grandfather pastored for more than thirty years. His mother, his father, and his siblings had attended that church. I didn't want to interfere with their family tradition, so I felt it best that Terry made the decision regarding the church that we would ultimately join.

For four Sundays in a row, I stood there, hoping that Terry would want to join the church.

On that fourth Sunday, he grabbed my hand and whispered in my ear, "Do you want to join this church?"

"Yes, if you want to."

I wanted to sprint to the alter so that we could shake Pastor Clark's hand before Terry decided that we shouldn't join. I gave him a piercing gaze with a radiant and heartfelt grin. He then escorted me to the altar holding my hand. This moment will always be one of the most cherished moments in my life.

In our first three years as GMZ members, Pastor Clark delivered God's Word, bestowed new wisdom, imparted truths that we had yet to discover, and guided us at a pace most comfortable for our individual growth. Under Pastor Clark's leadership, I witnessed God developing our prayer life, as partners, by leading us to pray, to praise, and to worship God together as well as during our personal time alone with Him.

Since Terry had not been accustomed to praying as partners in his previous relationships, he had reservations when we began praying together. After praying together for two or three years, his hesitation subsided while his participation grew. He even led some of our prayers, which encouraged my heart and gave me even more hope for a brighter and secure future together. He had grown from a spectator to an active participant.

What an achievement to have Terry join me in prayer as a prayer partner! But with every accomplishment, lurking in the shadows stood a disappointment, such as Terry yielding to the temptation of an occasional foray into smoking crack, not because God didn't give him a way out or an escape from the temptation, but because he was not ready to let go of the strongholds that kept him from trusting God. But the progress that I observed kept me focused and grounded because I saw greater progress and growth between each episode of him yielding to crack. Each time he failed in resisting temptation, God used it to build his resilience, ensuring that a fall would not prevent him from rising again.

The premise here is that we all fall, but we can also rise. And in rising, the lessons learned strengthen our ability to recognize and overcome obstacles, preventing them from holding us down or causing extended recovery time or greater harm.

During the early stages of the aftermath, the most notable outcome of our prayer life resulted in Terry developing more desire for stability. Quite often, I suggested to him that he needed a stronger motivation to resist drugs to avoid falling for every temptation that the enemy threw his way. Though this made sense to him, choosing to use drugs trumped not using drugs.

Terry's failures to resist the temptations could overwhelm me with grief because God remained constant in bringing to my mind the fifty or sixty times over the years that I had attempted to quit smoking and how part of me still wanted a cigarette from time to time. I found myself wandering around in areas where people were smoking. If I hadn't wanted to smoke, I would have stayed away from areas where I knew that others would be smoking, but because I wanted to smoke and didn't want to admit it to myself or out loud, I made it a point to stroll by a friend who smoked or pass by the designated smoking areas with the hope of bumming a cigarette from a fellow smoker.

I lied to myself, as Terry lied to himself. Just as I manufactured opportunities to smoke, he too found opportunities to use. And when I threw caution to the wind and days later purchased a pack of cigarettes,

Terry did the same. He ended up using crack for a day or two, as compared to the weeks or months that he had gone in the past.

Focusing on the progress that Terry had made remained critical to maintaining faith strong enough to overcome the enemy's attempts to break me, though this proved difficult at times. Regardless of what happened around us, God always lured me in, at a minimum, with a glimpse of progress.

For example, six years into my relationship with Terry, he had not shown any interest in joining his dad on Sunday mornings to assist him with his Sunday morning radio show. My father-in-law had built a successful radio announcing show and had performed as an announcer for more than thirty years.

I had always thought that Terry's personality echoed his dad's personality. And working with him on his show would have seemed natural for Terry, but during the entire time that we dated, Terry rejected the idea. I never understood why he did not hold an interest in being on the radio with his dad.

Occasionally, Terry assisted his dad when he performed as the master of ceremonies for shows that he produced and brought to Austin, but still, he didn't pursue following in his dad's footsteps. In 2004, he appeared on his dad's radio show, the first time that I heard him speak out through the radio waves.

Terry had not bought another car of his own since the Toronto had been repossessed, so I drove him to his parents' home so that he and his dad could ride to the radio station together. They had to arrive at the radio station by 4:30 a.m. to prepare for his dad's show, which started at 5:00 a.m., in order to smoothly transition from the previous announcer's program. Once at his parents' home, I resumed sleeping until 8:00 a.m. I then cooked breakfast for his mom and me, and together we listened to Terry and his dad on the radio.

This was the first time that his mom and I listened to the show together; her face lit up with amazement at how much Terry sounded like his dad did fifteen or twenty years ago. We both couldn't have been prouder of Terry. Terry being on the radio that day presented additional evidence of his progress and God's potential plans unfolding. Though so much more needed to be unveiled, on that day, at that moment, what I heard proved to be enough to keep my hope alive and to strengthen my faith, and I'm sure Terry's as well.

God seized every opportunity to help us grow. In addition to working at Fast Park, the City of Austin's Solid Waste Department, now known as Austin Recovery, hired Terry to work as a Solid Waste Operator in September 2005. And, at the end of August 2005, the great city of New Orleans suffered a catastrophe named Hurricane Katrina and found itself underwater. My entire immediate family, my mother and father, my three sisters and their husbands and children, and my youngest sister's mother-in-law and sister-in-law, relocated to the Austin area as they weathered the devastating effects of Hurricane Katrina. Twelve of my family members stayed with Terry and me. At 24 years old, Erika worked as an apartment manager and had her own three-bedroom apartment, and she opened her doors to my youngest sister, Monya, her husband, her mother-in-law, and her sister-in-law. Many of our neighbors, friends, my co-workers, and our church family showed incredible generosity to my family, and to this day we are appreciative and thankful beyond words for their kind hearts and deeds.

In my family's time of need, so many people joined Terry and me in helping them, but God also used them to bless us. One of the opportunities that God seized made possible for Terry to experience, firsthand the loving, close-knit, and resilient family I came from, deepening his connection with me and giving him greater insight into my upbringing.

Living so far away from my family had, up to that time, limited Terry's ability to see my interactions with my family for more than a week or two at a time, but Hurricane Katrina presented the opportunity for him to see our interactions beyond those weeks, after the novelty of distance and absence wore off.

The values and principles by which my sisters and I had been raised introduced him to a behind-the-scenes peek at the Thomas girls. He saw that respect, encouragement, comfort, and empathy stood as the backbone of our (the Thomas girls) connectedness, which included the connectedness to their spouses and in-laws. Even if we didn't agree with one another's decision, our upbringing called for respect. And if such decision-making didn't work out as expected, we consoled and lifted each other up from the disappointment.

And God, in his infinite wisdom, even made way for Terry to see the relationship between my family and Erika's dad, whose refuge from Katrina became Austin after initially being transported to Idaho. He saw my family show respect toward him irrespective of the role that he played or didn't play in Erika's life. They treated him the way that they would want to be treated and the way that they felt that God would want them to treat him. My bond with Terry constituted one union, one flesh, as instructed in the Bible, which is what my family practiced in all sincerity.

> *Therefore, a man shall leave his father and mother and be joined to his wife, and they shall become one flesh.*
>
> Genesis 2:24 (NKJV)

Living in such close proximity solidified the genuineness of our relationships. It built a more cohesive bond between Terry and me and between Terry and me and the other members of my family. It helped him to see the similarities and the differences between our upbringings, which enhanced his ability to trust me more. As a result, he revealed more of himself and unveiled a deeper part of his being. For many, Hurricane Katrina devastated them and tore down their entire worlds, but for my family and me, Hurricane Katrina bestowed blessings upon us and presented a time of building closer relationships.

On the morning of October 18, 2005, Terry received a call from one of his siblings informing him that his mother had passed away.

Standing in the bathroom door, he leaned into the bathroom. "Get dressed. Mama passed away."

I can recall the night before having a dream where I heard angels singing, *Hallelujah, Hallelujah*. Hearing the news of my mother-in-law's passing reminded me of my dream.

While riding in the car to the hospital, my father-in-law announced on the radio that his wife had passed away and, in an instant, he exited the airwaves. When we appeared at the hospital, we noted that family and friends had gathered on the floor of the hospital where her body lay waiting for loved ones to bid their farewell. Terry and I entered the room where she lay and approached the bed. I touched her arm and whispered good-bye.

I then walked away from the bed, leaving Terry alone with her to commune with her in the privacy of his own thoughts. As I meandered away from the bed, I was drawn to the window, and I looked up at the sky as if I could catch one last glimpse of her. This called to mind a dream that I had about her in 2000. In the dream, she appeared to me as an owl. As I gazed out from the second-floor window of the house I inhabited in the dream — a house unlike the apartment I rented in waking life—she flew toward me and perched on a tree branch just inches from the window. Though she took the form of an owl, her true identity was unmistakable to me.

I spoke to her with a soft voice. "Mrs. Martin, what are you doing up here?"

She uttered, "I'm here to let you know that it didn't hurt. It just burned; it burned a lot."

She then flew away. Twenty feet away from me an unknown substance, which I imagined to be her spirit, fell from the underside of her owl-shaped body, and then she vanished.

As I stared out of the hospital window, engrossed in my thoughts, reminiscing about the dream that I had had of her, one of my sisters-in-law tapped me on the shoulder, letting me know that my father-in-law had entered the room. I left, feeling more alone than ever despite the gaggle of family and friends lingering outside of her hospital room. I cannot recall Terry's whereabouts at the time. I longed to escape, so I proceeded to the elevator and found my way to the parking garage. Out in the parking garage, I saw Terry's uncle, Reecy, sitting alone, smoking a cigarette.

Eight months prior to Mrs. Martin's passing, I had decided to stop smoking for good. I felt that I couldn't expect Terry to break his habit if I didn't even attempt to break mines, once again, so I prayed for God to eliminate my desire to smoke. In response to my request, I felt the Spirit of Jesus beckon me to step out on my imaginary water in the same way that He instructed Peter to step out of the boat onto literal water and walk toward Him.

> *"Lord, if it's you," Peter replied, "tell me to come to you on the water." "Come," he said.*
>
> Matthew 14:28-29 (NIV)

In my spirit, I stepped forward and took his hand. At that moment, I stopped smoking. But with Mrs. Martin's passing and the emptiness that I felt, I yielded to temptation and bummed a cigarette from Uncle Reecy. Temptation never takes a vacation.

Mrs. Martin's passing broke my heart into a million pieces. As the first person to embrace me and confirm that God had sent me to help Terry, I cherished and treasured her. God had to have revealed His purposes and intentions for me to her. And she, without reservation, communicated to her close friends and family her intuition and discernment because when she introduced me to others, it felt as if they had known me for years. They had heard so much about me, yet I had not heard a word about them. Mrs. Martin lent herself to me as a sounding board to toss my innermost feelings regarding the difficulties, disappointments, victories, and my relationship with her son on. I poured my heart out to her, all of my feelings of pleasure, hurt, anger, and contentment. I felt like she helped me balance my stress levels. Her spirit calmed and comforted me when I needed it most. And with her passing, I felt even more alone and could not see anyone to replace her, not a single person, connected to my daily plight, to ease my fears in her stead.

Sometimes my feelings of anger may have hurt or bewildered her, but over time I'm convinced that she realized that my ranting acted as a mechanism for relieving myself of some of my own hurt and bewilderment. At the end of the day, I am certain that she knew the level of commitment I felt and that I had shown that my love and intentions toward her son were honorable. Before she left this earth, she knew without a shadow of a doubt that I loved her son and would be there for him. In fact, according to Terry, she had instructed him to hold on to me no matter what.

Terry and his mother had a close relationship, which pleased me because I have always felt that the relationship between a son and his mother is an indication of the relationship that he will have with his wife. Seeing the interaction between the two of them inspired me to encourage and push Terry as much as possible to visit and spend time with his mother. I admired their relationship and the interactions between them because the picture that it painted for me exhibited evidence of how he would treat me in my old age and perhaps in days of sickness and poor health.

It also portrayed God's love for me. He loved me so deeply that He sent a Savior to redeem my soul, and, in His perfect timing, gave me a husband He knew would love and care for me when I needed it most. I am touched and relieved that Mrs. Martin's last memories of Terry had him well, working for the City of Austin, for nearly a year, and available for her during her last days.

By the end of December of 2005, all family had left to go back to New Orleans or some surrounding area to begin the rebuilding of their homes, except my mom and dad, who left in January of 2006, to rebuild their home. During the entire time that my family stayed with us, Terry stood strong and sober, including during one of the hardest times of his life, his mother's passing.

After my family left, Terry and I purchased a yellow Labrador from one of my co-workers and named her Sasha. Two months later, two of our friends, Tony and Maryanne, purchased a Cadillac for Terry because

Terry indicated to Tony how much he admired one he had seen at a nearby dealership. Not knowing Terry's history with cars, they did not realize the harm that purchasing the vehicle could cause for him. And quite honestly, by that time, my confidence had grown some because he had been sobered for over two years.

In January of 2006, our daughter Tera gave birth to our first grandson, Carrell. In May 2006, Terry had another off to the races episode that ended in his arrest. While Terry served his jail sentence of four months, Erika gave birth to her first son, Gabriel. Three months after Gabriel's birth, Terry completed his jail sentence and returned home.

Terry's May of 2006 off to the races episode was a devastating blow to my heart and an embarrassment to my ego because I thought that he had overcome his addiction, and this episode cost him his job with the City of Austin. I worked in Human Resources, and many of my acquaintances who worked in the same department in which Terry worked now knew that my husband had an addiction, and that embarrassed me.

However, to my good fortune, the two people, senior manager and the human resources professional of his department, with whom I had built close relationships with, understood and offered their assistance to save Terry's job, but because he had failed to follow proper protocol for situations such as his, they could not help him.

Terry worked as a Solid Waste Operator which required him to have and maintain a Commercial Driver's Licenses (CDL). Since he possessed a CDL, options for addressing drug-related problems could have been sought had Terry followed the proper protocol which was to bring his drug issue to the attention of his human resources personnel. They considered his failure to notify them of his drug problem, along with him not calling or showing up for work, to be failure to follow proper protocol and job abandonment. Had he contacted them, they would have offered him an opportunity to enroll in a rehabilitation program and, if completed, he could have resumed working in the same capacity in which he had been working prior to enrolling in the rehabilitation program.

Hurt and anger consumed me. In a fury I pawned my wedding rings. His wedding ring had already been lost when a so-called friend stole his pawn ticket during a previous episode of him running off to the races and retrieved his ring without his knowledge. He acted as if our marriage and what we had built together didn't matter, so I decided that I no longer wanted to wear the rings that symbolized our marriage.

After Terry's episode in May 2006, he called to inform me that he had been arrested; and asked me to arrange for the Cadillac to be towed from the location where he had left it. I did have the car towed, but not to my house. Instead, I had it towed to Tony's house and told him that the car would no longer belong to Terry. Tony showed genuine sympathy for what had happened, and I assured him that he should feel no regret or remorse because all blame fell on Terry and not on him or Maryanne. I promised him that their act of kindness engendered sincere appreciation from Terry and me. Two to three months later, Tony sold the Cadillac.

When Terry was first hired by the City of Austin, he had requested a reduction in his work hours at Fast Park, which meant that he worked part-time at Fast Park and full-time at the City of Austin. When he was arrested, in addition to losing his job at the City of Austin, he lost the Fast Park job as well. After being released from jail, he contacted the manager at Fast Park to see if she would re-hire him. To his surprise, he was indeed re-hired.

Terry's customer services skills have always dazzled the manager of Fast Park. She relied on his performance when company dignitaries visited the lot, so re-hiring him did not present a problem for her at all. She also had a relative who battled with drug addiction, and her ability to relate with Terry's situation—through her own experience with her relative's drug addiction—enabled her to fully embrace the favor and grace God had placed on Terry.

As an ally to Terry in his fight against drug addiction, the disappointment when he yielded to his temptations to use drugs sucked the wind right out of me. Just when I thought that our lives had moved forward, that the issues with his drug addiction were in the past, that our future was bright, and that Terry walked in his deliverance, free from drug addiction, BAM! A bullseye smacked me right between the eyes. I learned a painful lesson, to never lower my shield of faith during spiritual warfare and not even in the aftermath.

From September of 2006 through the end of 2011, the aftermath continued. Terry and I decided to rededicate our lives and be baptized a second time. Since we had both been baptized as children—without fully grasping the true meaning of baptism—we felt it was important to make a conscious, adult decision to accept Jesus as our Lord and Savior. So, in October 2010, we were baptized again, this time with full comprehension of the commitment we were making.

Close to twelve years had passed since the breaking of the yoke. Even though significant progress had been made, we still suffered through a hiccup or two here and there. But for the most part, Terry's spirituality grew by leaps and bounds, which strengthened his capacity to evade and avoid the wiles of the devil. He craved greater spiritual growth and a life that enabled him to be dependable, consistent, productive, and profitable. He yearned for a life that enhanced his ability to be the man, husband, father, and grandfather that God had intended him to be.

I recognized and witnessed the fulfillment of the desires that Terry always spoke of. He listened to progressive preachers and motivational speakers who sustained him, kept him moving forward, and anticipating positive outcomes. His hunger for God's word shone through his eyes, but from time to time he succumbed to his urge to use drugs.

The major difference between the beginning of the aftermath and this period of the aftermath was that the time that Terry spent away using drugs decreased from days to no more than a day or an overnight stay. Though Terry relied on God, his most prevalent reliance was on himself. I had mentioned seeking help outside of himself and God, but that option didn't resonate with him. He kept rejecting that idea. So, while we did see progress, total deliverance had not yet occurred. In fact, Terry continued to drink and smoke. He continued to think that he could stop smoking and drinking at any time, yet this remained sometime in the distant future.

During the aftermath, friends that had chosen the same lifestyle as Terry passed away from physical ailments and/or complications from alcohol and drug abuse. I'm sure that reflecting on the memories of these close friends had to have had an impact on his view of his own mortality.

Two of Terry's closest friends, Woods and Jackson, were like brothers to him and brothers-in-laws to me. Both rallied behind our relationship. They always encouraged him to do better and to be stronger. Sometimes, they saw him while he was on one of his runs, and they persuaded him to call me and let me know that he wanted to come home.

One effect of yielding to temptation was that Terry always felt a huge bombardment of guilt and condemnation. Though Jackson and Woods each had their own addictions, along with failing health, they saw excellence in Terry, if he could ever break free of the drug addiction that bound him. I know that he misses them, and to us they are not forgotten.

Since we had reached the milestone of twelve years into the aftermath, the time had come for exercising more faith in Terry's growth and development. Though we both harbored our fears related to Terry purchasing a vehicle, we had to ensure that our faith outweighed our fears, so in August of 2011, Terry and I decided to buy a truck. He purchased a 2002 Chevy Silverado 1500, black, two doors with a cabin. The engine, the body, and the reasonable price impressed Terry the most.

This new truck would be helpful to us if he used it as an asset and as a means for him to be more independent and productive. With this truck, Terry could increase his ability to earn money, responding to opportunities such as hauling material or using it for transportation to a part-time job, rather than as a liability that caused hurt, anguish, and unnecessary setbacks. I prayed, stepped out in faith, and trusted in God for greater peace. I did receive assurance that no matter what happened, God would not put on me more than I could bear.

In the summer of 2012, my father-in-law, Mr. Martin, got sick. During his recovery, Terry promised him that if his health improved and he resumed his radio program, Terry would transport him to and from the radio station every Sunday. In the fall of 2012, he recovered and resumed airing his program, and as promised, Terry picked him up and dropped him off at the radio station every Sunday. Terry also felt a need to transport him to and from the radio station because, at that time, an epidemic of younger adults attacking, or what they called clocking, the elderly had been occurring in the Austin area during early morning and/or late-night hours.

After Terry transported Mr. Martin to the radio station two or three times, he noticed the difficulty that Mr. Martin had carrying his bags of music CDs up a flight of stairs to the broadcasting room, which was located on the second floor of the radio station. Terry then decided to assist his dad with lugging his bags up to the broadcasting room. This avoided any potential strain on Mr. Martin's back.

By the end of 2012, Terry had decided that he would stay throughout the broadcast to assist Mr. Martin with whatever he might need. Not long after that, Terry participated in the radio broadcasts with his dad. Mr. Martin's radio audience had become accustomed to hearing both of them on the air.

After a year of being on the radio with his dad, Terry announced to both his dad and me his interest in becoming a radio announcer. I found it hard to contain myself because Terry had finally come full circle. I watched him go from having no interest in it, to considering it, and finally, to a complete commitment. This thrilled me, as he had such a natural talent for it.

I imagined that Mr. Martin wanted his legacy to be handed down to Terry. I recall Mr. Martin confiding in me that he wanted to pass his legacy to one of his children, but he would not push it because of the level of commitment required. He felt that the decision had to be made by the individual, and that if the decision to pursue radio announcing as a career ever materialized, he would offer whatever assistance he could to ensure his child's success.

One of the greatest impacts that I observed in Terry's life, during the aftermath, derived from Ron Carpenter. Thinking back on my first time hearing Ron Carpenter, Terry and I were both feeling lazy and relaxed, and we watched as Terry flipped through an enormous number of television channels looking for an interesting show or movie to watch. He landed on a channel that was airing Ron Carpenter.

I could not have been more amazed and intrigued as we watched him. He taught the word of God with such a style and skill that I had never seen before from other pastors. As he interpreted and articulated the word of God, I imagined God talking and walking alongside him.

The revelations that he presented penetrated into the deepest corners of my mind and my heart. I thought to myself that all that pour out of him in his sermons had to have descended from the throne of God. In that sermon he focused on the role of woman versus the role of man. He talked about how God created women to be relational while men were created to be more linear.

From that day forward, I tuned in to Ron Carpenter and learned that his teaching style favored teaching in a series rather than in individual stand-alone sermons. He informed his audience that he preferred to research, organize, and focus on all that God thinks, instructs, and speaks on in the Bible about a particular subject and present it as a collaboration of God's thoughts, instructions, principles or keys, and commands on a subject or topic.

I have enjoyed his teaching style and themes ever since that day when Terry accidentally found him on TV. I've enjoyed themes such as *What Makes a Man, What Makes a Woman, Mind World, Enemies, Distinction, Chosen, Supernatural, Growing Pains,* and so many more. Ron Carpenter became a household name in our house, so much so that both Terry and I invested in his ministry.

Terry ordered a monthly subscription called The Vault, which is an online platform that gives access to a collection of Ron Carpenter's sermons, teachings, and other exclusive content. The Vault is often used by individuals looking for spiritual growth, biblical knowledge, and practical insights on topics like faith, relationships, personal development, and overcoming adversity.

And I pledged to give a donation to his ministry. Ron refers to his donors as partners because every donation partners with him to spread the gospel throughout the nation and around the world. Both of our commitments are considered minimal prices to pay for the teaching and growth that we gain from Ron Carpenter's ministry.

Through Ron Carpenter's ministry and his style of teaching and preaching, Terry grew to embrace the need for both hearing and knowing the Word of God. Ron Carpenter's ministry engraved on his mind and in his heart the importance of knowing and digesting God's Word. Ron impressed upon Terry that he could not hold God to His Word if he didn't know God's Word.

Ron even addressed father-son relationship dynamics and the importance of open communication, mutual respect, and attunement in resolving relational issues. In this particular sermon series, he emphasizes that healthy relationships often demand a willingness to forgive and engage in honest conversation, even when it is difficult. In addition, he discussed how many father-son conflicts arise from unmet expectations and/or misinterpretations, misconceptions, and confusion.

After watching this sermon series, Terry realized that the time that he spent with his dad had been anchored in his commitment to join him at the radio station. He recognized the significance of being there, which opened them to strengthening their bond and developing their relationship beyond the traditional father-son roles, growing instead into a genuine friendship. This time together generated a vast number of opportunities to talk about any issues that may have hindered or that may be hindering their relationship.

As time passed, I saw a new closeness in Terry's relationship with his dad. In fact, I even saw a shift in my relationship with Mr. Martin. He noticed and acknowledged that I loved his son and that I didn't desire to control him but wanted him to blossom into the man God wanted and intended for him to be. I believed that God intended Terry to be a man who could stand on his own, confident in his abilities, and strong in his will to be a man of God.

I don't know how many times he thanked me, over the radio, for being a wife who stood by his son, was devoted to his son, and trusted his son to be the son he needed to be. Once, he conveyed to me that many women wouldn't agree to their husbands leaving their beds in the wee hours of the morning to take their fathers anywhere. And for that, he had immense respect and admiration for me.

Terry aired on the radio with Mr. Martin from September of 2012 to April of 2014, when Mr. Martin passed away. Terry had not used crack cocaine during the entire time that he aired on the radio with his dad. After hearing of Mr. Martin's death, fear crept into my mind. I wondered what would happen now if Mr. Martin were not there for me if an episode occurred. Just that quick my faith had been confronted. I recall thinking, *God, what are you doing?*

Mr. Martin's death surprised me.

Terry called me at work and announced, "Viv, daddy's gone."

"Gone where?" I assumed that he meant that he had gone out of town because he traveled often.

"He's gone."

"I heard you. Where did he go?"

"Gone, gone."

"You mean he died?"

"Yes."

What a shock! I notified my manager that I had to leave, and I met Terry in the parking lot where I worked. We rode to Mr. Martin's house, where family and friends had already gathered.

I felt lost and, to some degree, abandoned. Outside of God, I felt like I had no other allies. I had been on this assignment with Terry for so long that I felt that the novelty of the mission had worn most friends and some family members out, so I refrained from calling them every time a new incident arose. Except, Mr. Martin. *Now, with him gone, what will I do? What will Terry do? And what will we do?*

Terry stood strong. He worked with the radio station to pay tribute to Mr. Martin and his years of radio ministry. People called in from all over the nation. I had no idea the extent and magnitude of Mr. Martin's fame. I couldn't have been prouder of Terry for participating with other radio announcers in taking calls from artists offering their condolences and fond memories of Mr. Martin as a tribute and homage to his lifelong work and accomplishments.

After Mr. Martin had been laid to rest, Terry received news from Mr. Martin's station manager that the radio station had been sold, and that Mr. Martin's show had been cancelled. What a blow to Terry. Both he and Mr. Martin had hoped that Terry could carry on his legacy. In fact, Mr. Martin had already talked to his station manager about it.

Not long after Mr. Martin's passing, an opportunity or two presented themselves to Terry, but neither of them materialized. Terry remained optimistic and kept the faith that one day God would open the door through which He intended Terry to go.

Between Pastor Clark and Ron Carpenter, Terry and I took giant strides forward. Terry's familiarization with the Word of God increased, thereby enhancing his confidence in praying for both him and others.

After Mr. Martin's death, Terry and his siblings managed Mr. Martin's affairs, and Terry used his portion of his inheritance to upgrade/renovate our home in preparation of selling it so that we could move to the home in which we planned to retire.

In late summer or early fall of 2015, Terry's childhood friend's father passed away. After seeing his friend at the gravesite, Terry reunited with him later that week, which led him to use crack cocaine, after he had not used it for almost two years. A rapid spiral downward led Terry to lose almost two years of sobriety.

We had gone through so much, and after all of the growth and the progress that he had made, following and applying the teachings of Pastor Clark, Ron Carpenter, and the Word of God, I couldn't wrap my mind around him deciding to go backwards causing him to relapse.

This decision tore at the very fiber of my soul. The disappointment, hurt, anger, and every other emotion that I couldn't necessarily name brought tears pouring from within me. It felt like tears of blood gushing from my veins. The anguish that built up inside me refused to go away.

Terry had achieved too much success and had received too much of God and His strengthening principles for him to act helpless, as if he had no power to resist any of the wiles of the devil. He knew that whenever temptation presented itself, God always gave him an opportunity to escape it, but this time he failed to take the escape route. Instead, he surrendered to the temptation. Terry ended up disappearing for three days, pulled three thousand dollars out of his bank account, and went on a crack binge. Blessed as we were, we had already completed the upgrades and renovations to the house, so the money that he spent didn't impact our moving plans.

So many times, in the past, I thought in my head that I had had enough of this roller coaster ride with Terry. But now, for the first time, my heart spoke within my spirit, *Enough*! And for the first time, I heard God agree. *Yes, enough! He must now choose who he is going to serve.* I knew that these were the exact words spoken by Joshua to the people.

> But if serving the Lord seems undesirable to you, then choose for
> yourselves this day whom you will serve.
>
> Joshua 24:15 (NIV)

So, we had finally reached the place where the rubber meets the road. We had come to a crossroads, and we would find out whether all of the years spent traveling on this road of addiction, fighting in the spirit, for Terry's life, had been in vain. He had to decide now because, for me, walking away had escalated from a mere thought to a near-reality. But, before I took that hike, I felt the need to reach out to Pastor Randall Franklin, the minister who had married us, and his wife, Cynthia, to discuss my feelings and options.

I couldn't hold back the tears. "I have had enough. I cannot go through this any longer. I am tired. Enough is enough. I wanted our marriage to work, but I cannot not deal with his addiction any longer."

Randall and Cynthia listened to me in an attentive and empathetic manner. I felt genuine concern and love from them. After hearing my brokenness, they both ministered to me by quoting scripture and words of wisdom.

"Viv, Terry needs help with his addiction. He cannot do this on his own. He needs to seek professional help." Randall generously offered his insight.

He then hugged me, and the three of us prayed. I left there feeling uplifted, but I knew that I had to be willing to let God do what I couldn't do. I realized that sometimes I could be a hinderance by not surrendering and giving in to God taking over when circumstances and the situation demanded such. I was guilty of trying to handle my circumstances and situations instead of letting God handle them. If God wanted my relationship with Terry to be successful and endure, it would be up to Him to do what He knew to do.

Upon Terry's return from the three-day bender in 2015, I presented his choices to him, which were either to go to rehab in another state or stay in Austin and live his life however he wanted. But this did not include me because going backwards didn't work for me. I had found that endlessly repeating or continuing down the path of drug addiction made no sense to me and that that journey had come to an end for me. I informed him that going to rehab in town was not an option. He needed to go to rehab in a place where he had never been before for a minimum of two months.

He resisted, but he could see that this choice would define the rest of his life, with or without me. He knew that the path that he had taken had ushered him into a choice that would end his relationship with me and destroy the life that he had built until that moment.

I knew that this choice wouldn't be easy for him because it meant exploring territory that he had never explored before. He would have to leave Austin and stand on his own. He had no idea what awaited him, and because of that, it was natural for fear to take over. I didn't know what choice he would make. What I did know, however, is that change had to happen.

Terry decided that he would go to rehab, and he told me that he wanted us to have dinner with all of the kids, the grandchildren, and his siblings before he left so that we could spend time together and pray as one united family. Terry selected the rehab to which he wanted to go, and he called the facility to speak with a counselor.

While the counselor had him on hold, Terry used this as an excuse to have me hold the phone while he and our third grandson, Isaiah, went outside to retrieve Isaiah's bookbag, which had been left in Terry's truck when Terry picked him and Gabriel up from school earlier that day. While Terry was outside getting Isaiah's bookbag, the counselor returned to the line. I informed the counselor that Terry had gone outside for a minute.

Isaiah returned, but Terry did not. I checked outside, and he had left. I told the counselor what had happened and hung up the phone. Terry had made his decision, and I had made mine. I decided to move forward with my life without him.

After three days, Terry returned home.

"Terry, I'm done. You need to pack your belongings and leave."

He replied, "I made an appointment at a facility called Serenity Rehabilitation Center (SRC) in Michigan. I will be leaving on Tuesday, April 5th."

This gave him two days to prepare for his trip. His first priority was him calling his manager at Fast Park to inform her of what was happening. She offered him encouragement and told him to let her know how she could be of assistance to him.

The rehab facility that he had selected paid for his plane ticket. He needed to buy a suitcase and some other items that he planned to take with him. He also sold the car that our son, Terrance, had given him before Terry bought his truck—a car Terry once said he planned to fix up someday. He used the money he received from the car sale to retrieve items that he had pawned to purchase crack so that he wouldn't lose them before returning from Michigan.

On the morning of April 5, 2016, I dropped Terry off at the airport so that he could board a plane bound for Detroit, Michigan. From the airport in Detroit, he would be picked up and shuttled to Serenity. Because I worked at the airport, I met him on the secured side, which meant that I didn't have to go through the Transportation Security Administration (TSA) security checkpoint. I could wait with him until he boarded his plane.

All kinds of thoughts ran through my mind, and I'm sure that thoughts ran through Terry's mind as well. Despite any fear that I may have felt, I felt proud of him for taking this leap of faith. I could see uncertainty in his eyes, but the way that he held his chin up spoke to the courage and hope that gave him the strength to move forward with what he hoped would be the beginning of a new life for him.

"Boarding Detroit, Michigan," a man blared through the overhead speaker.

Terry gave me a heartfelt hug that felt like he wanted to hold on to me for dear life and kissed me like he had never kissed me before. He tossed his carry-on luggage over his shoulder and strode toward the line to board the plane. I followed him. Tears welled up in my eyes, but I fought the urge to cry. I wanted him to know that I would be okay, that I would manage our household affairs in his absence, and that we would see each other soon. As we stood in line for him to board the plane, we looked into each other's eyes, whispered I love you to one another, kissed one last time, and then he moved forward into the jet bridge.

I prayed that he would have a safe trip, and that God would take care of him. As I stared from a distance, the jet bridge door closed, and he vanished. I proceeded to my office. By the time I made it to my office, he texted me and informed me that his plane had already pulled onto the taxiway and that he would call me when he landed in Detroit.

Let your faith be
bigger than your fear.

CHAPTER ELEVEN

RECOVERY

"Hey, babe, I've landed, and I'm in the van, en route to the rehab center. I'm not sure where it is. The location is not shared with new residents."

Relieved to know his status, I yelled, "Thank God, you made it!"

"I'll call you after I've checked in and get the layout of how things are gonna work."

"Okay."

"I love you, Cuddles. I'll talk to you later."

My mind took me back to when he first called me Cuddles, twenty years ago. Not long afterwards, I dreamed up three endearments by which to call him, all of which have lasted throughout our time together, Sweet the Wheat, Sweets, and Sweetie.

"I love you too, Sweet the Wheat."

Hearing that Terry had made it to Detroit eased my mind about the flight. My next worry, about which I needed reassurance, was the legitimacy of the facility and its effectiveness. I had never heard of that particular center, and the state of this world made it difficult for me to trust the claims made by any facility.

Later that night, Terry called me and gave me information about how to contact the center, if I needed to. Most of our conversation that night focused on what it would be like when he returned home. I encouraged him to concentrate on sharpening his life skills, seeing life from a new and different perspective, and experiencing a new place. Being his first night, the difficulty and fear that he felt was expected and logical. Like many other endeavors, it was typical for the first night to be the hardest. Deep inside, I knew that he would adjust to it and that he would absorb the lessons that he had enrolled in that facility to learn.

A Serenity representative contacted me to take care of the business end of his stay there. She gave me the contact number for his counselor and the address of the facility, in the unlikely event that I should need it. Terry's insurance considered addiction to be an illness, which enabled him to use the Family and Medical Leave Act to protect his job. I worked with his manager at Fast Park to ensure that she received the necessary paperwork. She offered her encouragement and requested that I let Terry know that she wished him well.

I discovered that having Terry at rehab was quite demanding for me. I missed him, but I knew that this was what was best for him. During the first week of his absence, I focused on work. I started my workday early and often stayed late. I needed a distraction to keep my mind off of his absence, and I prayed for his well-being. Outside of work, I meditated day and night on God's Word.

After the first week, I adjusted to Terry's absence. In fact, I felt relieved. I reclaimed a peace that I hadn't felt since meeting Terry. I no longer worried about him. I knew that his safety was at least temporarily assured and that God's protecting hands held and comforted him. Contentment and confidence in the process persuaded me that his choice of facilities would meet his needs and with God's help would produce a new and improved man. I knew that this too, this time apart from Terry, would pass and that he would return in two months, but I didn't want him to rush the process by returning too soon. I wanted and needed him to have a life-changing experience.

After two weeks in the facility, he sounded better. He talked about home, but he did not focus on being home. He talked to me about his need to participate in the programs and the process as much as he could.

And he made a commitment to do so. My heart swelled with pride in that moment. It filled my heart with joy and gladness to know that he had surrendered and decided to embrace the help that he had initially fought.

He talked to me about the check-in process and the Substance Abuse Treatment Inpatient Rehabilitation Program, which would offer him care, therapy, and support. Through his program he could participate in the 12-Step Programs, which utilized the principles of Alcoholics Anonymous (AA) and Narcotics Anonymous (NA) and the support that those programs offered in the way of peer groups and sponsorships.

We talked about the other programs, such as the Mental Health program, where he would receive individual, group, cognitive, and trauma-informed therapy; the Physical Rehabilitation program that included focus on regaining and developing skills needed for daily living and working; and general wellness opportunities that involved healthy eating and exercise.

Terry talked about people he met from various walks of life. He mentioned the counselors who worked with him and other residents of the facility, who had become friends. Within my spirit, I experienced his connection and his commitment right along with him, and it exuberated me. What an amazing sound to hear in his voice the surrender of resistance and it become so calm, humble, and peaceful, in his mind as well as in his spirit. This sound brought a reassurance that God's work of deliverance had impacted him. I could visualize the physical manifestation of his addiction being conquered through the sound of his surrender. God had done what he had spoken of, and the physical manifestation of Terry's deliverance appeared to be almost at hand.

After being enrolled in the program for more than a month, Terry called. "Hey, Cuddles."

"Hey, Sweet the Wheat!"

"What are you doing?"

"I'm packing for my trip to New Orleans and the Smokey Mountains." I threw another pair of jeans into my suitcase.

"I wish that I could go with you."

"I know, but there will be other opportunities for us to go to New Orleans and the Smokey Mountains."

"Yeah, I know." He sighed.

"What are you doing?"

"I'm about to go to church."

My ears perked up. "What church are you going to?"

"There's a local church that residents of Serenity attend for Bible study on Wednesdays and for church services on Sundays."

The local church had about twenty-five hundred members listed on its roster. On any given Sunday a few hundred actually attended. A Serenity representative drove the residents who requested to attend the Wednesday and/or the Sunday activities and services to the church.

"Terry, I'm so glad to hear that you want to go to church. Do you feel that you're learning or growing from the pastor's sermons or teachings?"

"Oh, yeah, the pastor's sermons have given me insight that I never thought about or that I didn't think about in the way that he presented it. His preaching style does captivate me. I'm not bored at all. So far, what he has preached about has been relevant, interesting, and informative." Terry's enthusiasm came through loud and clear.

His enjoyment of church and the impact that the pastor's sermons had on him forced him to self-reflect and examine his own soul. He conveyed to me that he felt that his guard had lowered, and he didn't feel as vulnerable as he had in the past. He felt that his comfort zone had expanded, so he found himself opening up and communicating feelings and experiences that he would not have disclosed with the pastor or any other member of the church. His openness presented clear evidence of progress and growth. It also displayed a comfort level that he had discovered and accepted being away from home and connecting with others about his personal feelings. In fact, he stopped talking about wanting to be home and embraced his time away. When speaking of his return home, he framed it more as an inevitable event than as an utterance of longing.

He felt that he needed to be there, fully engaged, appreciating, welcoming, and anticipating growth.

Each morning, he woke up and broadcasted to the world at large, "Rise and shine. Give God the glory!"

At first, some people didn't take well to this phrase, but over time, he won them over, and they came to accept it. In fact, some of them reciprocated it by repeating it back to him. I've always known that wherever Terry goes, people are bound to love him because he's so lovable. His spirit is so genuine and contagious that anyone near him can't help but be drawn in by his kindness, thoughtfulness, and gentle nature.

Terry's time in rehab revealed God's intention to use his life experiences to help others. As I listened to Terry articulating to me the impact that connecting with God had on him and how it influenced him to be more vulnerable with others whom he felt needed the same assurance of God's love, forgiveness, and fulfillment that he had gained, I cried tears of joy. I marveled at how God could take one man's need for recovery and at the same time rejuvenate the life of a different man.

> But as for you, you meant evil against me; but God meant it for good...
>
> Genesis 50:20 (NKJV)

God had turned the desire for the evil addiction of crack cocaine into a driving desire to pass along the love of God to others.

> But God has chosen the foolish things of the world to shame those who think they are wise. And God has chosen the weak things of the world to put to shame the things which are mighty.
>
> 1 Corinthians 1:27 (NKJV)

This scripture reminds me that our minds are not like God's mind. We cannot grasp the mind of God. God's wisdom may appear to be foolish, but it has a deeper, more eternal purpose that worldly wisdom cannot comprehend. God uses the weak to illustrate that His strength is made perfect in weakness because when we are weak, we experience

God's strength through His power. The overall lesson for me is that God is everything to and for everyone, and in every situation, which is why He calls Himself I AM.

> *...Thus you shall say to the children of Israel, I AM has sent me to you.*
>
> Exodus 3:14 (NJKV)

On May 12, 2016, I flew to New Orleans for my 53rd birthday. This would be the first time in thirty years that I would celebrate my birthday in New Orleans. I planned a three-week vacation with my family. At first, I thought that it would be somewhat odd because of Terry's absence, but after the first night, I felt peaceful and at home.

The following evening, my sister, Shauna, threw me a birthday party, along with a party for her daughter, Arian's, upcoming graduation from New Orleans University's engineering program. Time with family felt so refreshing, and I welcomed every moment of it.

In addition to this celebration, my entire immediate family had planned a trip to the Great Smokey Mountains in Gatlinburg, Tennessee, during the second week of my vacation. Most of my family knew Terry's whereabouts, which explained his absence, but those who didn't know inquired about him. I didn't feel a need to lie because my family had always been there for us, and I knew that they would continue to stand by both of us. It brought me so much comfort knowing that I had a family that understood and cared for Terry and me during our time of need.

I recall the night that we gathered at my oldest sister, Deanne's, house to chill, and Terry called.

I announced to the family, "Wait, y'all, this is Terry calling."

The moment that I said hello, my brother-in-law, Talmadge, snatched the phone out of my hand and dashed out of the room. By the time that he had finished talking to Terry, the time granted to Terry by the facility had run out. Serenity allotted ten minutes at a time for each resident to talk on the phone. If no one else was waiting to use the phone, the resident could make additional ten-minute calls. If someone else needed to use the phone, the resident needed to honor that resident's allotted time.

Talmadge handed me the phone. "Terry's going to call you later."

I burst out laughing. This didn't bother me because I knew that he had missed Terry. In fact, everyone wished that Terry could be there, and everyone in my family was pulling for him and praying that all would be well with him. The transparent love that members of my family displayed without hesitation for Terry overwhelmed and humbled me.

Despite Terry's addiction, in all the years that I had known him, he had never communicated to me that he did not feel like a part of my family or that he felt that a member of my family devalued, belittled, patronized, or disrespected him in any way. My heart found comfort in knowing that my family recognized God's plan—that both Terry and I had roles in fulfilling it, and that their love was intentionally part of what God had designed for us. My family didn't hesitate to honor God's wishes by loving both of us. And for that, I am forever beholden to them.

Going to my hometown during Terry's recovery also supplied support for me. I found the Great Smokey Mountains to be gorgeous and captivating and the weather comfortable during the day and chilly at night. We stayed in the Westgate Gatlinburg Resort in Tennessee. I had a marvelous time sightseeing in downtown Gatlinburg, exploring the many eateries and browsing through an array of Christmas stores. We visited the Smokey Mountain National Park and saw Smokey the Bear from a distance.

Terry called while we toured downtown Gatlinburg, and I relayed to him the beauty of the exquisite town and my desire for us to plan a trip there in the near future. Terry and I travelled everywhere together, so I missed having him on this trip. He would have enjoyed being there with all of my family members. But I felt that though he may have missed this trip, God would create a situation for us where we could enjoy many more trips together in the future. My trips to both the Great Smokey Mountains and New Orleans ended sooner than I wanted them to, but I had to return to Austin for work. Though Terry could not go with me, I did have a wonderful three-week vacation!

The night that I returned to Austin from New Orleans, Terry called, and I discussed with him all that I had seen while on vacation. His genuine happiness for me and my enjoyment of my vacation time with my family spilled through the telephone lines and touched my heart.

I could hear his buoyed-up spirit in his voice and the delight that he felt about the connections that he had made with other residents and how comfortable he had become with his surroundings. His voice lit up even more when he described the field trips that he had gone on to a small city located near Serenity. He also spoke about what he had learned since being in the facility, such as focusing on speaking with greater clarity in confronting issues that bothered him, weight loss, healthy eating, and effective exercising.

Even when incidents occurred on my end, talking to Terry eased my burdens and helped me manage the strife. But if any of my issues disturbed him, he talked with his counselor about it, who then listened and helped him devise the best plan of action to address whatever needed to be addressed. He mentioned that one strategy that he had learned for handling difficult situations or resolving conflict involved addressing the trial or tribulation head-on rather than avoiding it. For some, confrontation feels natural, but for others, it can be so complicated that it becomes paralyzing.

During Terry's recovery time, receiving phone calls from those who cared about me and Terry brought delight and additional strength to me. Being in the corner of a person with an addiction is difficult, painful, and, at times, downright exhausting. The energy that goes into being there for a person who is addicted to drugs, encouraging them, enduring disappointments with them, and reaching for hope that seems miles away, are all gestures of support that the drug addict relies and depends on. This is why I've always considered myself to be a supporter in helping Terry through his addiction. My presence, love, help, and patience gave him the support that he needed. Though, in return, I too needed loved ones and friends to encourage and strengthen me.

I felt blessed and appreciative of the support system that God placed in my life to aid me in overcoming difficulties as they presented themselves. The aid that I received did not always derive from the most obvious places, either. Sometimes God used family, sometimes He used friends or even an enemy, but quite often, in my life, He used strangers.

An example of God using family is when Terry's brother accompanied me once or twice in visiting a crack-infested neighborhood to rescue Terry from the stronghold of the devil. He was Terry's only brother, and also, was the very one who told me on our first meeting date that God had sent me to help his brother. This assertion proved to be another confirmation of the role God had intended for me to play in Terry's life, though, at the time, I didn't know it. Another example of God using family and friends is when family and friends joined me in prayer and consolation. But the most unexpected support came from a stranger, and I found that to be most astonishing. I recall listening to the radio one day. The person speaking, without realizing it, embarked insight into my situation and circumstances related to Terry's drug addiction that soothed my mind and relieved me of worry and overthinking. He simply stated that everyone didn't see or know what God spoke to me or showed me so to ignore the nay-sayers because they have no idea of God's plans for my life. His words acted as confirmation for what God had placed on my heart earlier that day.

Other times, a person could have made a simple statement like *be still and know that God is God* or *let go and let God*. Even though I had heard both of those statements before, for some reason, hearing it from a random person at a random moment filled me with a sense of peace or confidence.

And let's not forget those enemies who may have thought to hurt me or who felt hostility, malice, or resentment toward me, but God took those ill wills to reveal His perspective on the matter, or He used their behavior as an avenue on which to usher in new hope. For instance, God used the negativity of some people I encountered to produce steadfast hope and faith by activating a natural stubbornness inside of me. It was like I had to proceed, hold on to God's hand, and stand firm because I had to prove that doubter and pessimist wrong.

If you are a supporter of a person with an addiction, there may be times when you don't feel the encouragement of others, which may make you feel alone, isolated, or ostracized by those whom you expected or hoped to be there to nurture you. Don't let this lack of aid or your perception of this lack of aid weigh you down. There may be many reasons for this.

One reason may be that these folks don't know how to support you because they're not familiar or knowledgeable about your situation, circumstances, plight, or struggles or they just don't know why you're doing what you're doing. When people don't know your why, it's difficult for them to wrap their minds around your cause, thus making it hard for them to offer authentic and heartfelt help.

In fact, others may become insensitive to your cause. They tend to make statements like the person with the addiction needs to straighten up, stop using drugs, and that the person who is a drug addict is doing what they want to do. Sometimes, they may accuse you of inflicting pain upon yourself because you should move on with your life and let the addict take care of themselves. Chances are that these people are not able to see what God is doing in your life or in the life of the person whom you're supporting. The lack of support from these folks might be in your best interests because listening to them may be more discouraging and exhausting than beneficial.

A second reason could be that the person upon whom you're hoping to rely may have been let down or hurt by the person you're supporting, a person connected to them, or even you. This disappointment or hurt might have caused them to become judgmental, bitter, or envious, which then keeps them from offering sincere or meaningful support. The story of David and Saul is descriptive of this scenario:

> *Now it happened as they were coming home, when David was*
> *returning from the slaughter of the Philistine, that the women had*
> *come out of all the cities of Israel, singing and dancing, to meet*
> *King Saul, with tambourines, with joy, and with musical instru-*
> *ments. So, the women sang as they danced and said, "Saul has slain*
> *his thousands, and David his ten thousand."*
>
> *Then Saul was very angry, and the saying displeased him; and*
> *he said, "They have ascribed to David ten thousand, and to me*
> *they have ascribed only thousands. Now what more can he have*
> *but the kingdom?"*
>
> 1 Samuel 18:6-9 (NKJV)

Saul's anger, feelings of hurt, and envy impacted the rapport between Saul and David, despite David's wholehearted display of love toward Saul and Saul's family, without David even knowing why. Further on in the story, David inquired of Saul's son as to the cause of his estranged relationship with Saul, and neither did the son know why. David could not receive the type of leadership and sustenance or support he needed from Saul for reasons that were unknown to David. And like David, you may lack the support you need for reasons that are unknown to you. This is also true when there's unknown or unresolved issues between the addict and those whose assistance is being sought. In these types of situations, I contend that they're not personal and shouldn't be taken personally, because it will not hinder God's ability to deliver the help that you need elsewhere.

And third, it could be that people (your family, friends, acquaintances) don't always care about what matters to you. It's as simple as that. And that's okay because that's life. Some people care enough to be concerned about the plight of others, some people don't. They figure that they have their own problems and worries to tend to. Which is okay because if God wanted that individual to be a part of your support system, you could bet that somehow, someway, that person would be. Whatever and whoever God places in your life to assist you, be thankful for it, and utilize it to the greatest extent possible.

Supporters, there may be times when you feel that your direct connection with God is all that you have. It's you and God against the world, and there's no one else or nowhere else to turn to. Consider these moments to be real, tender moments. For me, these precious and private moments were when God's presence, protection, comfort, and Spirit overshadowed every negative feeling and left me in a state of peace and tranquility. During these times, it felt like God aggregated the sum parts of my being into His bosom.

It reminded me of the time when God called Moses into the mountain to give him the Ten Commandments, a set of biblical principles relating to ethics and worship, so that he could distribute them to the Israelites. I called these precious and private moments with God my *Moses in the mountain moments*, moments when I had never felt closer to God.

I don't know if you've ever felt God holding you, but I have. And in His holding me, I could feel an intimacy with God that spoke to my spirit, *You are my child, and I am your Father.* He wiped every tear from my eyes, like a parent wipes tears from a child's face and whispers, *It's okay, I'm here.*

Sometimes I could even feel a gentle rocking motion as I closed my eyes and slipped into a calm, peaceful sleep. And when I awakened, I realized that God had given me all the comfort I needed.

I must acknowledge that having Erika and Frank, her boyfriend, helped with bestowing a tremendous relief for me. They ensured that the housework stayed on track and made sure that I had food during Terry's absence. Having them there during some of my hardest days proved to be a true blessing.

Two days after I returned from New Orleans, Terry discussed Serenity's Aftercare and Support program with me for residents on the verge of completing their rehabilitation. This program gave Terry access to support groups like AA and NA and furnished continued access to therapy sessions, wellness check-ins, and sober living options or alumni programs.

In addition, Terry announced that he would be graduating from his program during the first week of June in 2016—he would then be two months free from drugs and alcohol. Though hints of elation floated in the air, a hint of fear and concern lingered about him as well. Almost two months had passed. Had he prepared himself to return home? Had he gained all of the necessary skills to navigate life without the structured environment in which he had been living in for close to two months? I felt anxious, and the butterflies in my stomach wouldn't stop. I thought about his first week in the facility and where his mental state had been at that time compared to our conversations now. I had witnessed through our phone conversations significant growth in Terry, so much advancement that it made me more faithful regarding God fulfilling what I trusted in Him to fulfill which was Terry's complete deliverance and recovery from his crack cocaine addiction.

When I talked to Terry about it, he stated that he felt ready.

"Are you sure that you're ready." I squirmed, sitting in the recliner in my living room.

"Yes, I'm sure."

"Well, your manager at work already told me, when I let her know the status of your program, that if you need more time, she has no problem giving it to you."

"Yeah, I know, but I am ready to come home."

For the remainder of his time in Michigan, I noticed that he seemed positive about what he had gone through, the people he had encountered, and the transformation that had occurred within him. Though he may have had some fear, which is typical under the circumstances, courage and confidence kept him focused on the broader picture, living the life that he wanted to live.

I had spent a great deal of time praying and strengthening my faith that all would turn out well for him and assuring myself that I would be okay too. During the two months of Terry's absence, I had grown used to not needing to care for anyone other than myself. I could choose whatever TV channel I wanted to watch, or I could leave the television off altogether. I could stretch out across the entire bed if I chose to, or I could lay in comfort in my usual spot.

The way that I had come to live my life would be different with Terry's return home. I would have to relinquish the space that I had become accustomed to having to myself. It's amusing how the human mind adapts to situations without much difficulty, especially those from the past. I had lived a single life for over thirty years before I married Terry, and in two months, my life had reverted back to my single life days. I used to joke with Terry about finding single life to be easier than married life, though, as a single person I did feel lonely at times.

After I maneuvered the lower-level traffic at Austin-Bergstrom International Airport to pick Terry up, there he stood waiting. The exercise that he had done had paid off. He appeared so slim and handsome standing there, his face radiating a bright, joyful demeanor. On June 2, 2016, my husband returned home from rehab, and I had to embrace and accept, without a shadow of a doubt, the idea that God sent him home recovered, whole, and ready to be the man God intended him to be. I bounced out of the car and hugged him. Words could not describe how it felt. And his kiss filled me with promise! And in an instant, I forgot all about the single life. I was so glad to have him home and to be in his arms. He made me feel safe and protected.

We ceased our embrace before the ground transportation crew could insist that we move on or issue us a citation. I hopped into the driver's seat of my car and steered the car in the direction of our home.

We conversed for five or ten minutes, and he informed me that he had seen one of our friends on his flight. I laughed because, no matter where Terry goes, he always sees a familiar face. It's the oddest coincidence. If Terry doesn't already know a person, he's bound to meet them and strike up a conversation. If they're in his company for long, he will have their phone number, promising to keep in touch with them. It's who he is. With Terry, no one is a stranger.

After laughing about Terry seeing a friend on his flight, we rode in silence for the rest of the way home. Terry gazed out the window and took it all in. I'm sure that it felt awkward for him. It always does when returning home after being away for a while.

Home, at last! Erika, Frank, and the grandchildren wrapped their arms around him, held him, and welcomed him home. And Sasha, our dog, jumped all over him once he walked away from the family's embrace. Two months away for us humans felt like a long time, but for Sasha, it seemed an eternity!

I sought the Lord, and he heard me…

Psalm 34:4 (NKJV)

….and he answered.

Psalm 34:4 (ASV)

CHAPTER TWELVE

ENJOYING A LIFE OF FREEDOM

After being home for three or four days, I could see a clear change in Terry's attitude. He was more self-assured and confident. He communicated with greater authority. He repeated with clarity some of the insights that he had gained in rehab, and I could see that he had absorbed the lessons that he had been taught. I had never been prouder of him. I prayed within my spirit that all of his steps would move him forward, ushering him to be who God had made him to be.

Terry's growth helped me to grow as well. On July 5, 2016, Terry quit smoking cigarettes. My first reaction to him quitting was doubt, as it had been in the past. *Yeah, right, we'll see. If he quits, I'll quit.* After seeing that Terry had quit for a week, I decided to join him and quit smoking myself, so on July 12, 2016, I quit an almost forty-year addiction to tobacco, cold turkey. I decided that I had smoked for long enough and whispered to God that my smoking days end today. And here we are nine years later, both of us are tobacco free, and Terry has maintained his sobriety from drugs and alcohol!

I wanted to visit a new church, First Church, in our neighborhood, but I didn't want to go alone, so I waited for Terry to come home from Michigan so that he could join me. Before visiting the church, I discovered that it was a part of the Pentecostal denomination. This pleased me because most of the churches that I had attended in the past aligned in some way with Pentecostal doctrine.

Two months after Terry came home, he settled into his job, and we agreed that attending a mid-week church service would be beneficial for us both, so we decided to visit First Church for the first time. The church congregation reminded me of settlers from the early 1900s, where tradition held strong and was closely followed.

The members greeted us as long-time friends and welcomed us in a manner that made us feel like special guests that they had been waiting for ages to visit them. The band played traditional Christian music, and the choir sung with enthusiasm and spirit-filled hearts. We enjoyed our visit so much that we attended services on Wednesday evenings often.

One of the aspects that I loved most about my experience with the Pentecostal denomination is its open praise and worship. Every Pentecostal church I've been part of has openly encouraged and practiced outward worship, where worshippers freely showcased their gratitude, love, emotions, and heartfelt appreciation to God. And this church matched all of the others that I had attended in this respect. I had grown accustomed to it, but it felt new for Terry.

In our attendance at First Church, God used this church experience and opportunity to teach Terry how to honor Him through unconditional praise. I witnessed Terry throwing up his hands and bellowing praises unto the Lord like he had never done before. I saw him kneel at the altar in surrender and honor the presence of the Lord. Before my eyes, I saw my husband take the steps and assume the posture of a conqueror with his head held high, his shoulders firm, and his feet planted solidly on the ground. He exuded unshakable power, as if God's glory had been poured all over him. There was no doubt in my mind that Terry's life had been reclaimed, and a new destiny given to him.

After attending First Church, a rootedness developed in Terry. Every day I could see his reliance upon God becoming more evident. He prayed more, and he referenced God more. His solution to every problem included him trusting God and acknowledging God, as commanded by God for his children to do.

> *Trust in the Lord with all your heart and lean not on your own understanding; in all your ways acknowledge Him, and He shall direct your path.*
>
> Proverbs 3:5 (NKJV)

I could see him hungering for God's word, as if he could not get enough of it. When he purchased Pastor Ron Carpenter's The Vault, we discussed the cost of it.

"Terry, it's $9.99 a month. Are you willing to pay that every single month?" I almost couldn't wrap my mind around him being willing to make such a commitment.

"Well, yeah! When compared to the amount of money that I spent on dope, $9.99 is peanuts, especially considering the overall benefit for me, and, well, for you too. All that we're going to learn, it's more than worth it!" he assured me.

And he proved to be right! In fact, we both use it. We both downloaded the Redemption app on our phones. Whenever either one of us want or feel a need to hear the word of God, we'll open our app, pick a sermon, and receive whatever message God may have for us to receive. I know that Terry enjoys having the app on his phone, and I enjoy having it on mine. Ron Carpenter has no idea the impact that he has had on Terry's life and on my life. It's remarkable how God works through a person, and they have no idea the influence that their words or actions have on another person's life. It is indeed a blessing and a miracle! It may be hard to imagine, but it happens more often than one might think.

From 2016 to 2018, we both experienced tremendous growth in our faith, in our comprehension of God's will for our lives, and in re-establishing and growing our trust in one another. Because of this growth, we decided to move out of the neighborhood in which we lived to the place where we planned to retire.

In early August of 2018, we put our house on the market. It stayed on the market for thirty-three days, forcing us to move into a rental house while we built our dream house.

We moved into a rental house in September 2018. I found living in the rental house exhausting because with most of our belongings being in boxes or in storage, finding what I needed when I needed it raised my stress levels beyond my comfort zone. It felt like every time I needed something, it either sat in a box or was in storage. And, of course, if whatever happened to be in a box, it was at the bottom of a pile of three or four other boxes. Having access to a limited wardrobe also proved difficult, as I had to dress in business attire at work. Though we experienced discomfort, anticipating the move into our new house made it all worth it.

Caledonia Builders, the construction company we used to customize our home, scheduled us for a March 2019 completion date, but because they ran into a drainage issue called a swell, which is a small rise or mound in the land's surface, they had to delay our completion date. Though this type of drainage issue is quite common, it blew their construction budget out of the water, but they did make the correction and reset our completion date for July 2019.

We visited the construction site every other day. I found it fascinating to watch how our house came together and to see all that went into its creation. From selecting the lot to choosing the floor plan, making decisions at the showroom, and the actual construction, each step felt remarkable! For me, the most incredible part was how the water would pump and be distributed throughout the house. Ron Carpenter once preached that the stuff not seen is what is real and will last for all of eternity.

It rained every single day during October. In November, it rained every other day. And in December, it rained at least twice a week.

In January of 2019, the rain slowed down; it rained every other week. At last, in the middle of February, the builder poured the slab. We also found out from one of the construction workers that the rain in the previous months had been God working on our behalf because all the rain helped with the re-directing of the swell. It turned out that the rain pinpointed where the new drainage path should be. We praised God for intervening, though we felt frustrated because of all of the delays. But God being who He is, always right on time and working on our behalf, strengthened the efforts of the builders to ensure that the drainage problem had been resolved.

In March 2019, the builders built the frame of the house, and I felt like the exchange student, played by Eddie Murphy, in the movie *Trading Places*, who when the train commenced moving, he claps, *the train is moving, the train is moving, the train is moving*. By May of 2019, the putting up of the sheet rock enabled me to see each individual room. The house no longer resembled a stick house.

Our dream house is 3,468 square feet and includes four bedrooms, four and a half bathrooms, a formal dining room, an open-floor kitchen and living room, an office, a laundry room in the middle of the house, an upstairs movie/game room with its own full bath, and a three-car garage. The house sits forty to fifty feet from the street and has a long driveway. We also have a nice-sized backyard that we can view from a wrap-around patio.

Though this thrilled me, I could see how overjoyed Terry felt. I noticed through Terry's eyes that God had revealed to him His power and ability to transform brokenness into a strong temple, ready and waiting to be filled with blessings.

> *But as it is written: Eye has not seen, nor ear heard, nor have entered into the heart of man the things which God has prepared for those who love Him.*
>
> 1 Corinthians 2:9 (NKJV)

This scripture solidified Terry's faith that God is all powerful and could do whatever His heart desires. It helped Terry take ownership of his identity in Christ and the plans that God had for his life. He figured that if God could bless us with the house, he was certain that God could bring to fruition the plans that He had for him.

> *"For I know the plans I have for you," declared the Lord, "plans to prosper you and not to harm you."*
>
> Jeremiah 29:11 (NIV)

Watching Terry's reaction fascinated me. It sparked my imagination to the point that I envisioned a flower blossoming in the early morning dew while radiant rays of sunshine adorned it with the softness of the morning sun! For me, it brought unspeakable joy and pride. I thought to myself how awesome it would have been if his mom and dad could have seen his transformation and felt the joy that I felt.

The further that we got into the construction process, we then visited the property two or three times a week, praying that God would steady and lead the hands and the hearts of the builders so that our house could be completed with as few flaws as possible.

Right after the walls had been completed, we invited our Greater Mount Zion (GMZ) — Circle of Greatness (COG) family out to pray and worship with us. The COG concept derived from the book of Acts. These are small groups of ten to fifteen people who meet weekly to connect with other church members.

Because our church has at least six thousand members, if not more, on its church roster, these small groups are an excellent way of getting to know one another and are in alignment with biblical teachings found throughout the book of Acts. These small groups gather in homes or other settings and, with today's technology, online, for fellowship, prayer, and teaching. The members of the small groups are people from all walks of life who join to explore the Bible, engage with one another for drawing from each other's experiences and personal stories, and to build acquaintances and friendships for developing and maintaining a healthy spiritual life.

For Terry and me, through the COG, we have gained reliance partners or people on which we depend as we navigate through the many ups and downs of living, all while strengthening us along the way. And in doing so, it feels like our pleasant days have outweighed our unpleasant days. For in our pleasant days our reliance partners celebrated with us, and in our unpleasant days they helped carry our burdens through prayer and encouragement.

This COG meeting occasion marked one of our most fulfilling moments as we offered thankfulness and gratitude and we submitted requests for blessings. We moved through the house, room by room, ensuring that prayers extended to every space and the entire property. Our COG's presence, love, and fellowship touched our hearts and illustrated the importance and true impact of having this small group in our lives. And afterwards, we ate a meal at one of the local restaurants.

We closed on the house in the second week of July. We moved in on the weekend following the closing. What an incredible and extraordinary feeling! Words could not describe the gratitude that we felt every time we thought of God bestowing such a blessing upon us. I wanted to keep pinching myself to see if I would wake up from the fantasy.

We purchased our first bedroom suite, and it made us feel like the king and queen that we are. For all that God had given us, I knew that He would help us to sustain it. He would give us the means, including the energy needed for the upkeep and beautification of both the house and the almost one-acre of land.

Being in our new neighborhood has also been a much-needed enhancement for our family. The peace and quiet have brought us an inordinate calmness. I love strolling through the neighborhood and taking in the beauty of God's creation, the green trees and creeks flowing with water tucked away in the valleys and in the hills. I've even caught Terry deep in thought, gazing into the backyard scenery as if he was gazing into the wild as the deer fed on berries scattered across the hilltop.

By Labor Day, most of the organization inside the house had been completed, though much work remained to be done both indoors and outdoors. Curtains had yet to be installed, and rugs had not been laid down. Landscaping needed more attention as well. However, we had ample time ahead of us, and we approached each task one step at a time. After all, we had our entire lives to complete it.

We planned to have an official housewarming party on the weekend after Christmas, and we invited all of our family, friends, and neighbors, and our pastor, Gaylon Clark, to officiate the blessing of our home. But because Terry's family already lived in the area, we didn't think that they should have to wait until Christmas to see the house, so we decided to have a sibling housewarming and invite our children and grandchildren and Terry's siblings and their children.

Erika, Frank, and a friend I met while working at the City of Austin, Tony, cooked for the occasion. Terry had to work, so Tony stepped in to do the grilling for us. What a blessing for us that he agreed to step in for Terry. So, with Tony on the grill, Frank frying fish, Erika cooking baked macaroni and cheese, baked beans, and corn on the cob, and Tera, our second to oldest daughter, contributing her rendition of guacamole with chips, we had a grand feast. My contribution to the menu was dessert; I bought cheesecake and cookies.

We had a wonderful time, and all who attended exhibited overwhelming joy for Terry. They rejoiced over the work that God had done in his life, and genuine gratitude and joy were reflected on each face, alongside gratefulness to God for the transformation that He had brought about in Terry's life.

God had heard the prayers of many and produced Terry's deliverance, freedom from addiction, spiritual growth, and He had blessed me with tremendous faith. In December 2019, we gave glory to God when Pastor Gaylon Clark officiated the formal dedication of our home. With the blessings of Pastor Clark, our COG family, members of both of our families, and our friends, celebrated and basked in the blessings that we received from God. Though others may not have experienced our exact journey, they knew our story, so they could rejoice with us. All who attended could say that they had known us when.

And that is the kind of God who Terry, my family, my friends, and I serve, one who takes our weaknesses and shows us that He is more powerful than those weaknesses. In addition, He takes our unparalleled courage, resilience, resolve, and fortitude and shows us that He is mightier and more dominant than them all. These attributes that God possesses alone are worth praising Him beyond measure because for those who are supporters of drug addicts, this truth blesses them with the endurance to walk mile after mile, stand day after day, and to rise to their feet every time.

As supporters, God's word instructs us that we must not grow weary while doing good.

> *And let us not grow weary while doing good, for in due season we shall reap, if we do not lose heart.*
>
> Galatians 6:9 (NKJV)

> *But those who wait on the Lord shall renew their strength; they shall mount up with wings like eagles, they shall run and not be weary, they shall walk and not faint.*
>
> Isaiah 40:31 (NKJV)

> *...the race is not to the swift, nor the battle to the strong...*
>
> Ecclesiastes 9:11 (NKJV)

> *But he who endures to the end shall be saved.*
>
> Matthew 24:13 (NKJV)

So, I encourage every supporter to hold on to God and His teachings. I promise that He will be the I AM (all that you need) that He promises He is. Never forget that God's mind is not your mind. And whatever the outcome, He is working it out in your favor. True faith is believing not what can be seen but what cannot be seen. It is knowing that in the end God's Will shall be done, and however it works out, it is what God thinks is best.

And last, but not least, a simple and powerful word from God gave me the peace that I needed. Without it, I do not think that I would have made it. So, I'm leaving it with you, and I pray that it brings the same power to you that I received.

> *Be still and know that I am God.*   Psalms 46:10 (NKJV)

This single scripture, calmed my mind, focused my soul, and released my spirit to embrace the peace necessary for me to exhibit true faith and trust in God.

This word from God speaks of encouragement, confidence, and promise in their simplest terms. When the mind is still and not overcome or overwhelmed with uncontrolled thoughts, it enables silent moments for God to be heard through His whisper and for His peace to be felt. And accompanying peace is calmness, acknowledgement of God's presence, and trust, which is God's ultimate desire for His children.

I'm convinced that in all of life, the most vital expectation for all of God's children is to love without conditions.

> *And now abide faith, hope, love, these three; but the greatest of these*
> *is love.*
>
>   1 Corinthians 13:13 (NKJV)

As children of God, when we love, we're proving that our representation of God goes beyond knowing Him. It signifies that He indeed created us in His image because God Himself is Love.

Whether it be the ways that I've seen love or the places where I've encountered love or the people who I've loved and by whom I have been loved, the one common denominator has been God's love, which He had declared may never be taken from me.

> *For I am persuaded that neither death nor life, nor angels nor prin-*
> *cipalities nor powers, nor things present nor things to come, nor*
> *height nor depth, nor any created thing, shall be able to separate us*
> *from the love of God which is in Christ Jesus our Lord.*
>
>   Romans 8:38-39 (NKJV)

Below is a poem that I wrote to convey my view of God's love. It's my attempt to depict who God is, who God has always been, and who God will continue to be. His word is true, and His love lasts forever...

Love Is...

Love is God in all His splendor,
Giving and caring without being hindered.
Loving when love doesn't come in return,
Yet, being patient as His children learn.

Love is man with all his strength,
Overcoming obstacles as they are sent.
Accepting the challenge to continue to love,
As he gives and shares his gifts from above.

Love is the wind as it blows through the grass,
Tilting and cooling the flowers while it pass.
Bringing freshness from the cleansing rain,
And a sense of freedom from whence it came.

Love is all things created by God,
No matter how common, no matter how odd.
No matter how big, and no matter how small,
Love is the image of God that resides in us all.

Love is...God.

I will bless the Lord at all times;

His praise shall continually

be in my mouth.

Psalm 34:1 (NKJV)